FILM STUDY IN HIGHER EDUCATION

HOPKINS CENTER, DARTMOUTH COLLEGE
Site of the 1965 National Film-Study Conference

FILM STUDY IN HIGHER EDUCATION

Edited by DAVID C. STEWART

Report of a conference sponsored by Dartmouth College in association with the American Council on Education

Published by AMERICAN COUNCIL ON EDUCATION

WASHINGTON, D.C., 1966

FILM STUDY IN HIGHER EDUCATION *is a report of the Cooperative Research Project No. V–007, conducted by Dartmouth College in association with the American Council on Education. The research reported herein was supported by the Cooperative Research Program of the Office of Education, U.S. Department of Health, Education, and Welfare.*

1785 MASSACHUSETTS AVENUE, N.W., WASHINGTON, D.C. 20036

LIBRARY OF CONGRESS CATALOG CARD NO. 66–22768

PRINTED IN THE UNITED STATES OF AMERICA

Acknowledgments

THIS REPORT is the product of a general inquiry which was initiated by a six-month preliminary study in 1964, an activity supported financially by the Motion Picture Association of America, Inc. The findings of the preliminary study, undertaken by the American Council on Education, were reported in the Winter 1965 issue of the Council's publication, the *Educational Record*. Two men were largely responsible for conceiving the original investigation: Ralph Hetzel, Acting President of the Motion Picture Association of America, and Lawrence E. Dennis, Director of the Commission on Academic Affairs of the American Council on Education. (Mr. Dennis is now an education adviser for the Ford Foundation in Venezuela.)

The following persons provided special assistance and advice in the course of the current project: Erik Barnouw, Ernest Callenbach, Andries Deinum, Jack C. Ellis, Edward Fischer, Robert Gitt, Orton Hicks, David Hull, Arthur Knight, David Mallery, Arthur Mayer, Margaret Twyman, Blair Watson (Associate Director of the project), Colin Young, and Edith Zornow.

The 1964–65 data on film courses found in Appendix D (reprinted from the *Educational Record,* Winter 1965) were obtained by Donald E. Staples, Assistant Professor, Motion Picture Division, Department of Photography, Ohio State University, and his wife Diane, using the format developed by Professor Jack C. Ellis of Northwestern University, who assembled the 1952–53 information on this subject. Chief credit for the bibliography is assigned to Jack Ellis. Information on film periodicals in the bibliography is reprinted from the *Catholic High School Quarterly Bulletin* (October 1965), an issue devoted entirely to film study, prepared by Reverend John Culkin, S.J., of Fordham University.

Contents

TOWARD FILM STUDY

by David C. Stewart

THIS IS A FILM-STUDY resource book designed to provide assistance to college teachers and administrators who plan to initiate courses in the history, criticism, and appreciation of motion pictures. Its contents will also be of interest to persons already professionally committed to teaching motion pictures as a contemporary art, since the descriptions of current film courses offer a basis of comparative analysis. In addition, this is a report on the current state of the art of film teaching in higher education; the courses chosen for description (five among hundreds now being offered) are at once unique and representative of others like them. The three critiques of the courses written by Professors Burchard and Young and the film critic Pauline Kael, also represent views which, while marked by distinctive expression, are not altogether uncommon in the academic community.

This is not a how-to-do-it book or a set of rules on film course construction. The five courses described by their teachers represent five different approaches to the study of motion pictures. Each is formed by evident differences in experience and temperament.

DAVID C. STEWART, editor of this book, has served as Director of the Dartmouth College/American Council on Education film-study project. He has been Director of the Washington Office of National Educational Television and Consultant on the Arts to the American Council on Education. He is presently Director of Educational Programs for the National Council on the Arts.

There is no description here of the history of film study in American colleges and universities. After studying the subject for nearly two years, we are of the opinion that such a history would not, at this time, prove either significant to education as a whole or useful to film study itself. Film teaching in elementary and secondary schools appears to lend itself more readily to historical treatment, perhaps because of its earlier beginnings and discernible trends, chiefly influenced by sociological factors.[1]

The appendixes contain information which should be useful to teachers who are new to film study. This material has been assembled largely in response to inquiries from teachers and administrators. We have been unable to list the name of *every* 16-mm. film distributor in the United States, but the major distributors are noted. The film distribution organizations and sources found in Appendix A provide films for the five courses which are described.

Background

The scene was set for the appearance of this report during a national conference on film study in higher education held at the Lincoln Center for the Performing Arts in New York in October 1964. The Lincoln Center Conference offered an opportunity to consolidate information gained during a six-month preliminary study of college and university screen education conducted by the American Council on Education.

The preliminary survey of this field was based upon three central assumptions: (1) motion pictures are a major, contemporary, artistic expression; (2) their cultural value lies far beyond pure entertainment; and (3) higher education, as part of its continuing

[1] A number of scholars have described the progress (and lack of it) of film education in American schools. Two recent examples are *The Study of Film as an Art Form in American Secondary Schools* (unpublished doctoral dissertation, Teachers College, Columbia University) by Stuart Selby, 1963; and *The History of Film Teaching in the American School System* (a lengthy article in *Screen Education,* Sept./Oct. 1965, a publication distributed in the U.S. by the National Screen Education Committee. *See* Appendix B) by Ronald Polito.

responsibility in the broad field of the arts, should contribute to the development of a more informed and discerning film audience.

Two of the major recommendations resulting from the 1964 conference were (1) a subsequent conference should be held to "consider the role of film-study courses in undergraduate and graduate education," and (2) "there is immediate need for the publication and wide distribution of a book which will describe, in detail, a variety of courses in motion-picture history, criticism, and appreciation, [reflecting] the broad range of current film courses of high quality. Such a book should contain the titles of texts and films used in the courses, listings of principal film distributors, and other information that would make it a valuable and useful reference source." The film-study project undertaken by Dartmouth College in cooperation with the American Council on Education, and supported by a financial grant from the Arts and Humanities Branch of the U.S. Office of Education, has addressed itself primarily to the fulfillment of these recommendations.

Film Study Today

Much has been learned about the study of motion pictures in American colleges and universities in the last eighteen months. Information obtained on this subject clearly indicates that although film study has made impressive advances in formal education during the last decade—particularly in the undergraduate liberal arts curriculum—much remains to be done before this academic inquiry enjoys accommodation in most institutions of higher education, to say nothing of being accorded full recognition.

The tables found in Appendix D describe a significant increase in the number of motion-picture courses since 1952–53. But in order to give the fullest meaning to these figures, they should be matched with similar quantitative studies of, for example, English literature or history courses. In light of the amount of informal but serious attention given to the art of motion pictures during the last decade, a time when the talents of European film directors were being enthusiastically applauded in this country, it seems curious that film study has not developed more rapidly. Some of the reasons are found in traditional resistance to curricular innovation. The popularity of movies, while serving to generate enthusiasm among students, has rarely enhanced films as objects of serious inquiry, particularly among teachers of more conventional subjects. Doubts about the "seriousness" of motion pictures as an art form have been raised by those who are otherwise liberal and sophisticated students of contemporary education. Some professional educators for whom the movies have always constituted an enjoyable pastime take strong exception to their inclusion in a formal academic program. Listening to the disquieted discussions of motion-picture study among academicians committed to the printed page as *the* medium of learning, one often recalls the line put into the mouth of a nobleman in Shaw's *Saint Joan:* "There is nothing more exquisite than a bonny book, with well-placed columns of rich black writing in beautiful borders, and illuminated pictures cunningly inset. But nowadays, instead of looking at books, people *read* them." It is disconcerting to some that nowadays, instead of simply looking at movies, students want to *examine* them.

But quite apart from these considerations, film study has faced major problems in pursuing its inquiry under circumstances conducive to achieving full understanding of the medium and developing sound scholarship. While motion pictures appear to be ubiquitous, especially in a society deeply committed to television, they are relatively difficult to come by for study purposes under controlled conditions. Present methods of film distribution are cumbersome and expensive. Current procedures for studying films, dictated largely by economic considerations (i.e., large classes in which each film is rarely screened more than once and is not available for review), rarely excite the potentials of intense personal study or research. This does not mean that excellent film-study courses are not offered, or that you cannot, as a student or teacher/scholar, examine films in a fully satisfying manner. It *does* mean, however, that until films for study purposes more nearly resemble books in terms of accessibility, a screen education in depth will continue to be a formidable undertaking.

In the preliminary report on film study, published in the *Educational Record*,[2] one of the central recommendations was: "Colleges and universities need to devise systems for circulating motion pictures among institutions within the same region for film-study courses, and develop cooperative arrangements for the acquisition and use of motion-picture classics." It was suggested that much could be learned from (book) library practices in these matters. It was also proposed that serious attention be given to the use of 8-mm., plastic, cartridge-load projectors which make use of film loops. Recognizing that a film made in 35-mm. is lowered in quality when transferred to 8-mm., it is nonetheless necessary to inquire how far this disadvantage may be compensated by a student's opportunity to borrow a film or a film sequence for projection, and study it at his personal convenience over an extended period.

A related problem is one which plagues both film student and teacher/scholar; namely, where to *find* films and information about them. To refer again to a recommendation of the preliminary study: "It is important to develop an information center for teachers of film-study courses. . . . Such a center might [provide] information on film rental and acquisition, annotation of major films, and a clearing house for theses and dissertations, as well as bibliographies of books and journals concerning motion pictures." Here, film study is seriously disadvantaged, comparatively, with "book study." No film reference work has yet been created which is comparable to the one libraries have in *Books in Print,* although the film council of the National Audio Visual Association (N.A.V.A.) has been authorized to publish—prior to September 1966—a resource guide to entertainment films. According to N.A.V.A., the guide will list available feature films in 16-mm.

[2] This and following quotations are taken from the article by David S. Stewart, "The Study of Motion Pictures in Colleges and Universities," *Educational Record,* Winter 1965 (Washington: American Council on Education), pp. 33–67.

and their sources. Approximately twenty-five thousand copies of the guide will be published and distributed free of charge to colleges, universities, and high schools through the United States.

It is apparent that the informational requirements of film teachers will grow increasingly acute in the months and years immediately ahead. If film study in American colleges and universities is to find a secure place in the undergraduate and graduate curriculum, some mechanism for exchange of information about motion pictures must be established. Such a facility could be shared with those who are professionally associated with pre-college film study (secondary school interest in motion-picture production and appreciation courses has been both vigorous and inventive) and the general public. It is hoped that the National Council on the Arts, which is presently exploring the possibilities of a National Film Institute, will incorporate plans to serve these needs. A National Film Institute might also concern itself with the accessibility (distribution and exhibition) of motion pictures for study purposes. While the formal and informal film-study requirements of this country differ in many respects from those in England and many Western European countries, much may be learned from the film institutes established in England, Sweden, Denmark, and France, to say nothing of those in Canada.

The preliminary film-study report commented upon nearly all major problems and requirements in this field: creating summer film institutes for training new film-study teachers; the development of a film-study information center; film distribution and the possibility of circulating motion pictures between institutions of higher education on a regional basis; the selection and translation into English of foreign books on films; establishing film artist-in-residence programs on college campuses; initiating studies to improve the technical facilities for storage, retrieval, and projection of films for study purposes; providing 16-mm. film distributors with accurate information concerning the basic motion-picture requirements (both complete features and excerpts) of film-study courses; and initiating programs of aid to young professional film makers.

Since the publication of the preliminary report some of these recommendations have found a response. There are some signs that the motion-picture industry and higher education may be approaching a better understanding of the relationship between film making and education. The Motion Picture Association of America has created a special commission on education which is, according to M.P.A.A., "designed to further study, research, and appreciation of motion pictures at various levels of education." The Federal Government supported a summer film-study institute at Fordham University during 1965. The first National Student Film Festival was held at the University of California, Los Angeles, in October 1965, under the auspices of the United States National Student Association, and there are plans to exhibit the winning films on campuses throughout the country. The World Law Fund has plans for a national student film-making contest, and it is anticipated that other such competitions serving to stimulate and reward new film-making talent will soon be established. These activities, and others like them, are central to the "film-study movement" which is presently characterized by a series of beginnings.

Informal Programs

This report is devoted mainly to the substance of college and university courses in the history, criticism, and appreciation of motion pictures. But such an account would be incomplete and inaccurate if it did not also include some reference to informal film programs which, while they may be unassociated with higher education's curriculum, are nonetheless the "cause" of many new formal academic courses.

There are nearly four thousand film societies in the United States; one and often more than one, on every campus. The quantity as well as the quality of motion pictures shown each year under their auspices is impressive. Smith College, for example, shows about ninety features every year and has been doing this since 1929. Dartmouth College has sponsored well over three hundred features and as many shorts in the last fifteen years. This is *in addition* to classroom use of films. The American Federation of Film Societies, described in Appendix B, has experienced a dramatic increase in membership during the past three years. A film society is often a student's first contact with an organized and serious interest in motion pictures. Active college film programs, however informal, lend support to curricular film programs in much the same way that museums and galleries supplement the work of art courses. Reference is made in Appendix C to the motion-picture activities of museums, libraries, and film archives. Most of these institutions are located near colleges and universities. The effectiveness of their programs, like those of the campus film societies, is difficult to measure, but there can be little doubt that their influence is considerable. Most museums maintain a film exhibition program. Many have broken away from strict attention to motion pictures *on* art and have begun to emphasize the study of films *as* art. The Museum of Modern Art in New York has provided much of the leadership in this field, but it is not alone in offering an informal film education to a large public audience. Some museums such as the Cleveland Museum of Art provide film appreciation series as well as informal film-making classes for children and adults. In addition, cultural organizations like the Institute of Contemporary Arts in Washington, D.C. regularly schedule film series treating motion pictures as an art medium.

Religious organizations, particularly Catholic groups, have been extremely active in creating film appreciation opportunities. An outstanding example is the National Center for Film Study established in 1962 by the Catholic Adult Education Center of the Archdiocese of Chicago. The Center serves teachers, students, seminarians, and the general public by conducting a variety of film education programs and providing study guides for about one hundred and twenty movies which have been termed by the Center "significant examples of various aspects of the film art." Professional associations within the teaching profession have shown considerable interest in fostering film appreciation. The National Council of Teachers of English has produced a book on the subject, entitled *Motion Pictures and the Teaching of English.* A permanent committee of the Modern Language Association, the Film Festival Faculty Advisors, acts as a forum for the discussion of problems of film rental and associated activities.

Individual films and film series which attempt to describe the nature of the motion-picture medium are not common, but those which have been designed to teach film appreciation are heavily booked by schools as well as colleges. One such series, created in 1965 by Professor Edward Fischer of Notre Dame University (a contributor to this volume), contains four 27½ minute films entitled *Elements of the Film, Visual Language of the Film, The Nature of the Film Medium,* and *Film As An Art.* The series, produced by OFM Productions in Los Angeles, is accompanied by notes entitled "How To See A Motion Picture" to be used as a study guide. Some measure of the interest in film study is suggested by the fact that, sight unseen, orders for the series were being received at the rate of three hundred each month shortly after its release. Some film series, less didactic than the one produced by OFM, have been developed for educational television stations. A notable example is the programs featuring critic Stanley Kauffmann, produced by Edith Zornow for noncommercial station WNDT in New York City.

While it has not been unusual for campus film societies to rent or borrow screening facilities from local commercial motion-picture exhibitors, few commercial exhibitors have, until recently, taken the initiative in booking a series of features revealing the work of a specific director, or describing a school of film making. However, an increasing number of individual exhibitors have established film societies, membership organizations with year-long schedules of private performances supplementing their regular movie fare. An example is the Janus Film Society operated by the

Janus Theatres (1 and 2) in Washington, D.C. Here, unusually interesting films (from the standpoints of history, theme, and artistic treatment) are shown each weekend on Saturdays at midnight and Sundays at noon. A recent program at Janus exhibited more than a dozen motion pictures created by new film makers including Kenneth Anger, Stan Brakhage, Robert Breer, Bruce Conner, Tony Rose, and Stan Vanderbeek.

In the Finger Lakes region of New York, officials of Schine Theatres have worked out a plan for an annual "International Film Festival series" with members of the faculties of Hobart College, Colgate University, and the State University of New York Colleges at Oswego, Cortland, and Oneonta. In each college town the local Schine Theatre manager, in consultation with a knowledgeable faculty member, books a series of exceptionally good motion pictures (once a month for a two-day run, for which a series of tickets is sold at a discount), and each film is followed by a discussion led by a college teacher. In most instances, these screenings supplement the regular college film society screenings.

Generally, these informal programs of screen education—in which college students are among the chief participants—rarely diminish the interest in formalizing film study by placing courses in the subject in the liberal arts curriculum. It would be too much to say that there is a direct cause-and-effect relationship between informal film programs and the establishment of formal film courses, but it is apparent that the activities mentioned above have greatly accelerated serious interest in film study in colleges and universities.

The Content of Film Courses

The prime concern of the Dartmouth College/American Council on Education Film-Study Project has been an investigation of the substance of current film courses in higher education. Film course content was the principal subject of discussion at the Developmental Conference held at Dartmouth College in October 1965, and it constitutes the major portion of this volume.

Considerable attention was given to course content during the preliminary film-study investigation, from May to October 1964. During this period, Professor Henry Breitrose of the Department of Communication at Stanford University made a survey and analysis of representative courses in motion-picture history, criticism, and appreciation. His report, delivered at the Lincoln Center Film-Study Conference on September 22, 1964, was summarized in the previously mentioned *Educational Record* article, "The Study of Motion Pictures in Colleges and Universities." In addition to Professor Breitrose's investigation, the preliminary study project director collected descriptions of courses through interviews and correspondence with approximately sixty teachers prior to the start of the Dartmouth College/A.C.E. film-study project. The Breitrose analysis and the assembled course content material became the foundation of the twelve-month study and exercised an important influence upon the selection of course descriptions found in this book. A distinguished panel of teachers advised the director in the final selection of courses which were first described in papers presented and discussed at the Dartmouth Conference, and subsequently edited for publication in this report: Erik Barnouw, Columbia University; Andries Dienum, University of Oregon; Jack C. Ellis, Northwestern University; Edward Fischer, Notre Dame University; Arthur Knight, University of Southern California; Blair Watson, Dartmouth College; and Colin Young, University of California, Los Angeles.

A careful re-examination of the film course material collected during the preliminary study and a review of similar data (syllabi, bibliographies, and film lists) compiled in the course of the twelve-month project has confirmed the validity of Professor Breitrose's original analysis and the usefulness of his definitions of general course categories. Briefly stated, the major course categories (or "approaches") are described as follows: (1) *Histori-*

cal, often relying on the survey series of films available from the Museum of Modern Art and on the standard film history texts, with considerable attention to significant names and dates. A survey approach is often employed, examining the significant periods of film making in various countries. (2) *Comparative-aesthetic,* or "and film" approach (music and film, dance and film, the novel and film, and so forth), achieving what Professor Breitrose refers to as "a patina of academic respectability" in consequence of its origin in older and more entrenched arts. It is similar to aesthetics as taught in departments of philosophy in that a number of art films are dealt with. (3) *Functional,* representing a synthesis of the historical and the comparative-aesthetic, together with a unique quality, a consideration of both history and aesthetics as tools rather than ends. The functional approach regards film as a unique art form, requiring no justification, disguise, or excuse in terms of other art forms. Its primary concern is how film (and individual movies) operates, i.e., how it is put together and why it uses certain kinds of content, approach, and strategies of structure.

As the preliminary report recognized, within each approach there is a wide range of course content and many differences in the manner in which courses are presented. While the courses selected for description in this book reveal many of these differences, they clearly emphasize what Professor Breitrose terms the functional approach and a preference for the consideration of film *qua* film. This is perhaps due to a strong commitment to film as an art form on the part of the five teachers, born of their experience as film makers and critic/historians. Generally, those who teach film courses are closer to the creation of their subject than teachers in other areas of the humanities—art history, for example, or literature. Among the contributors to this book, George Stoney is a distinguished documentary film maker; Hugh Gray has written film scripts for every major studio in Hollywood; Professors Fischer and Ellis have had considerable film-making experience within the university structure; and Arthur Knight is a professional film critic and historian with a large national following.

It is of more than incidental interest that such film teachers, once having constituted a majority of all teachers in the field, are now in the minority. And there is every indication that they shall remain so for a long time. In other words, film teachers who are "essentially" film makers or film critics are being joined by teachers of philosophy, drama, art, history, speech, literature, and music who take a genuine (but often rather peripheral) interest in motion pictures. It is a condition which the first group finds worrisome, and with good reason. There is no present equivalent in film study of the American Educational Theatre Association, or the Speech Association of America, or the College Art Association, or other organizations which seek, at least indirectly, to set standards and qualifications for teachers in these fields. The Lincoln Center film-study conference in 1964 and the Dartmouth conference in 1965 may have signaled the beginnings of such an organization; indeed, the central recommendation from the latter meeting was a strong request that another conference to discuss film study should be held at the earliest opportunity.

Those who prepared descriptions of their courses for this resource book had particularly difficult assignments. They were asked to provide information on all texts and films used, and to indicate the sequence in which subject matter was discussed. Beyond the *what* of the course, moreover, they were prevailed upon to provide a description of *how* they taught, and *why.* The results emphasize the large difference between providing information and communicating the essence of creative teaching. Teaching, like many highly creative processes, resists literal description. For many teachers, the only satisfactory explanation of how teaching and learning happen lies in the act of teaching itself. One of the best ways to discover how a teacher communicates information and knowledge enthusiastically is to become a student in his class.

Still, as unrevealing as some of the course descriptions are with respect to their *how* and *why,* they managed to excite heated discussions at the Dartmouth conference. This is a reflection of deep interest in the subject as well as the temperaments of those who are professionally associated with film study. It is no discredit to the sensitive and articulate people who have pioneered motion-picture study, to observe that the intellectual and emotional entanglements generated by discussions of course content sometimes form patterns of an intricacy that would have impressed the Byzantines.

A review of the proceedings of the Dartmouth conference, during which the courses in this book were discussed, reveals two dominant themes: (1) a plea for the orderly and disciplined development of film study, and (2) a warning that the study of motion pictures is in danger of accepting "formalism" and a "methodological approach" which will inevitably reduce student enthusiasm and interest. The papers presented by Professors Burchard and Young and Miss Kael became the focus for much of this discussion. The following quotations have been taken out of a much larger context but as representations of discussion themes they are not untypical:

> Film study doesn't mean only the development of taste but the increase of knowledge as well—scholarship. I think the reason film teachers are so sensitive on this issue of scholarship is because they do so little of it.

> Something is wrong if . . . we have to find a *method* of teaching. We teach the way we teach because we have a certain experience and have responded to certain things in films.

> I hope you do more than create first-rate training for the next generation of film makers. I think film is as important as it is because it can *save* us from another academic speciality which we have enough of now. Don't make this another academic discipline that is "respectable."

> I think this flaying the academicians is a red herring. It comes up at each of these meetings. [The film teacher] must accept the responsibility of being an academician. It is not beneath us or beyond us to do scholarship and research.

> I'd like to enter a sincere and earnest plea that methodology never enters the film courses.

We run the risk . . . of taking the native interest that kids have in movies and sterilizing it, and making it 99 44/100 percent pure, so we can grade it and put it into books. Film ought to be taught in universities in terms of the excitement and surge of interest of the kids who take these courses.

Mr. Fischer's presentation is very valuable because he intends to set up objective standards of approaching art. Most people's attitude toward art is entirely subjective. They feel intensely about it but when they try to say anything beyond "I like it very much" and "I dig it" and so forth, they have nothing more to say. Students, unless given some objective guides, have nothing to say except a few little platitudes.

The notion that a person has to be in love with the particular films that he teaches about, although it's a nice idea and in some places it creates a greater climate of enthusiasm on the part of the student, doesn't seem to me necessarily true.

Has anyone ever suffered from an over-enthusiastic teacher?

You suffer perhaps ten years later. You enjoy the class and then you realize you didn't learn anything from the teacher.

The place of film study in a liberal arts education may be somewhat precarious, but its continued presence seems assured. The dialogue between those who teach the history, criticism, and appreciation of motion pictures (much of which was begun during the course of these studies) is certain to continue in further symposia and conferences. The question of *whether* to teach motion pictures has been resolved affirmatively. The question of *how,* while it will never be answered to everyone's (perhaps, *any*one's) satisfaction, found the beginning of a definition in Professor Ellis' comment,

With such a rich medium, there is more than enough to go around. As long as it is taught with affection and respect, almost any approach can increase understanding and appreciation.

COURSE DESCRIPTIONS

MODES OF FILM COMMUNICATION

by Jack C. Ellis

"MODES OF FILM COMMUNICATION" which has been offered for the past nine years by Northwestern's Department of Radio, Television, and Film, is elected by students from other departments—notably, theater, English, philosophy, art, and journalism. Courses in film theory and history seem as appropriate within a liberal education as within a professional one.

In form as well as in content, film seems to have absorbed and therefore to reflect many of the most crucial aspects of what we call modern culture, so that one is ultimately led toward the dynamics of interaction between an extraordinarily lively art and its society. This course attempts to keep present realities to the fore. It includes representative as well as exceptional films and sets them within their economic contexts. At the same time it permits major emphasis on artistic matters. For students underexposed or impervious to aesthetic consideration of the older arts, the currency and excitement of film provide an attractive introduction to concepts applicable to the arts generally. So much is yet to be known about film that it would seem both willful and wasteful to ignore the

---

JACK C. ELLIS has directed the film program at Northwestern University since 1956 with two years' absence as a visiting professor at the University of California, Los Angeles, and New York University. He received his doctoral degree from Teachers College, Columbia University.

many established academic disciplines that bear upon it—philosophy, psychology, sociology, the history and criticism of the other arts. One may shudder at the danger of film being studied as an extension of literature, or as painting in motion, or as a reproduction of theater. But such a rich medium offers more than enough to go around. As long as it is taught with affection and respect, almost any approach can increase understanding and appreciation. "Modes of Film Communication" is an effort to suggest in one course many of the possible ways of thinking about film and some of the things that are known about it.

The goal of the course is to make students *see,* which D. W. Griffith urged as an ultimate creative function. This phrase seems to define even more precisely the function of education in relation to art. This aesthetic approach is also the one I care most about. It seems most basic to an understanding of film and most direct in its connection with film's evolving form, which has accelerated in its shifts during the past decade, tacking from drama toward the novel, and perhaps nearing a channel that will be recognizable as *film* to future film historians.

Mechanics

The course is offered every fall for one quarter—the beginning of a loose sequence, followed by "The History of Film" in the winter and by "The Documentary Film" in the spring. These critical historical courses are paralleled by a three-quarter production sequence, both series being preceded by a sophomore-level "Introduction to Film" and capped by a graduate seminar. "Modes" is open to juniors, seniors, and graduate students from any school or department of the university, without prerequisite. Enrollment has averaged twenty-nine over the last nine years.

The course carries four credits, meets four days a week, and consists of three fifty-minute sessions and one one-hour-and-fifty-minute session. Mondays and Tuesdays are devoted to a lecture interspersed with questions and comments. On Wednesdays the two-hour "laboratory" session consists of a screening, with each film briefly introduced to establish its setting and relevance to what we've been talking about and followed by immediate reactions and suggestions of matters to be dealt with the next day. Thursdays are given over to analysis and criticism of the films through class discussion.

The present text is *Film: An Anthology,* compiled and edited by Daniel Talbot and published by Simon and Schuster in 1959. The Talbot collection is valuable in outlining a variety of critical approaches and as a kind of annotated bibliography, with excerpts from the original sources serving as annotation.

The term project consists of a ten- to twenty-page paper on a single film—of any type, nationality, or period—not shown in class. The student must be able to see it a number of times.

The model for student analysis and criticism of a single film is suggested by the French film school, Institut des Hautes Etudes Cinématographiques, series of *Fîches Filmographiques.* Ideally each student becomes "the world's greatest authority" on his particular film. Approaches vary as widely as quality, and students sometimes apply not only research skills and insights developed during the course but the rest of their academic background as well. Aristotle's *Rhetoric* has been brought to bear on a series of TV commercials; Dreyer's *Ordet* looked at for its painterly qualities; *Golddiggers of 1933* studied as sociological document. The bulk of the paper is to consist of a close "reading" of the film, however, in terms of personal criteria (which the student is expected to make explicit at the outset) conditioned by the critical approach suggested by the film itself. The paper comprises half the course grade; examinations, a one-hour midterm and a two-hour final—a few long essay questions on both—the other half.

Substance

Each week of the ten-week quarter has its topic, but these topics fall into related groups. First, the three subindustries within the motion-picture industry are looked at separately—35-mm. theatrical, 16-mm. nontheatrical, and films for television. The underlying assumption is that the economic systems of production-distribution-exhibition as well as audiences and their expectations largely determine the quite different forms and contents present in each phase of the industry at different times and in differing cultures. Second, there is a four-week funnel-like sequence which begins with considerations of the philosophy of film and narrows down to its psychology, and to its technique. Two weeks are then devoted to an extension of the technique of film, and divided between the two main offshoots of the fiction film—the experimental film and the documentary. These two forms of the media, together with the fiction film itself, comprise film as an art form. Finally, in the tenth week we end with current developments and trends in the international theatrical film.

The course is described as a "beginning course at an advanced level" in film aesthetics (what film is) combined with a types-of-film survey (what kinds of films there are). At the same time it is acknowledged that we will also be concerned with the technological and business setting. In a course in literary criticism one doesn't go into the state of the publishing industry or the technology of printing, the merchandising methods of booksellers, or the interests and organizational affiliations of readers—though a case might be made for doing so. In film, however, the creative process itself is highly technological, much more expensive than printing, and the completed work is presented to groups rather than to individuals.

FILM IN THE THEATER—35-MM. The one-period discussion of the theatrical 35-mm. film industry revolves around an analogy between it and the automotive industry. As a film for this week we see a Hollywood feature from one of the popular and indigenous genres: a Western, musical, or crime melodrama usually. Last fall we saw *Ride the High Country,* and the class was sent ahead in their text (Warshow's *The Immediate Experience*) to "The Westerner." *The Gunfighter, 3:10 to Yuma, The Asphalt Jungle, The Set-Up,* and *It's Always Fair Weather* have also been shown. The first opportunity to establish criteria and method thus occurs with the most familiar.

FILM IN THE COMMUNITY—16-MM. Of the three subindustries, students are least familiar with the 16-mm. nontheatrical field. Though exposed to plenty of 16-mm. films as audio-visual aids, they've never thought about them as *film.*

As examples, last year we saw a film made to introduce the 1963 model Westinghouse refrigerator, a film enlisting support for the United Charities of Chicago, one designed to give deaf children practice in lip reading, another sponsored by the United States Information Agency, and one about pigeon racing. All were produced within the past two years by Northwestern students or recent alumni. The selection was not unrepresentative of the field, and stimulated questions of purpose and intended audience.

FILM IN THE HOME—TV. Film for television presents two convenient handles. One is a comparison between film and television as media of art and communication. The other is the steadily increasing interchange between the two, in material, personnel, and control.

Last year the showing for this session began with an assortment of commercials obtained from local television stations. Since these are the prime cause of the medium, a sampling is always included. Out of their natural habitat and with full attention paid, they provoke some valuable responses. The second example was *A Dancer's World,* about Martha Graham and her troupe, made by Peter Glushanok for the Pittsburgh educational television station. It is an extraordinary work in many respects, not the least of which is its blending of film, dance, television, and education. The American Cinema Editors' *Interpretations and Values*—the rushes and three editors' versions of a single sequence from "Gunsmoke"—

fits here because of its origin. Among the best of the films about film, it offers much to students at every level of learning, in technical as well as theoretical courses. *Grassroots,* the final film, is Denis Mitchell's study of Princeton, Kentucky, made for National Educational Television through arrangement with the British Broadcasting Corporation. It represents "Free Cinema" of impressionistic and highly selective observation, which is a style of personal film essay more or less native to television.

THE PHILOSOPHY OF FILM. There is now a shift to aesthetic matters embracing the total form. By this time students will have been reading Elie Fauré, Erwin Panofsky, Allardyce Nicoll, Susanne Langer, Parker Tyler, Arnold Hauser, Seymour Stern, Margaret Kennedy, John Grierson, James Agee, Robert Warshow, and Manny Farber.

Since most of my students lack the kind of grounding in the arts that perhaps can be assumed elsewhere, a common critical formula is outlined. It consists of four questions one might put to a film, or to any effort at communication or expression. Two apply to the use of the medium generally, to its "language"; two to the art work. First, to what extent does the particular film take advantage of the strengths and limitations of film form and communicate ideas and emotions that can best (or only) be communicated within it? Second, assuming a subject congenial to film, to what extent is the purpose accomplished? Third, if the intention is the creation of an art work, to what extent is a complete and unique artistic experience offered? Finally, to what extent does the work contain the qualities of brilliance, profundity, and universality that separate the large artistic accomplishment from the small?

These rather conventional criteria are applied to examples already seen in class and to other films with which students might be expected to be familiar, in an effort to render them less abstract than they may at first seem. To prevent attempts to use the four questions as a recipe, the class is reminded that these principles in themselves represent a particular critical preoccupation—what might be called formal criticism and is represented by Arnheim and Panofsky, among others, in their text. The experience and attitudes of each critic, it is urged, will suggest deletions, additions, and changes. Reference is made to other approaches in their anthology—the sociological, psychoanalytical, historical, comparative (film and theater, film and novel, film and painting)—as alternative aesthetic frameworks. Each film, students are reminded, is a unique statement, causing certain elements to be of prime importance in any consideration of it.

Having outlined a critical formula and urged modifications of it, a session is spent on the positions of two philosophical schools in relation to the arts and to film in particular. On the one hand there is the synthesis of ideas on artistic matters growing out of John Dewey's *Art as Experience,* which applies a number of concepts from modern psychology, anthropology, and Dewey's own instrumentalist philosophy to an understanding of the nature of aesthetic experience. On the other is the synthesis developed by Mortimer Adler and Robert Hutchins from Aristotelian and Thomistic aesthetics, set within a framework of classical-medieval metaphysics. These two philosophical poles seem still to exert the strongest influences on the study of humanities in American colleges and universities.

Susanne Langer has contributed perhaps the most widely valued development of what is here called "the Dewey position." Her major works bear directly on the nature of artistic communication. *Philosophy in a New Key* is subtitled *A Study in the Symbolism of Reason, Rite, and Art.* The later *Feeling and Form: A Theory of Art Developed from "Philosophy in a New Key"* has "A Note on Film," included in the Talbot *Anthology.* The other camp is fully represented by Mortimer Adler's *Art and Prudence: A Study in Practical Philosophy,* devoted to film. Not known as widely as it deserves to be and out of print for a good many years, *Art and Prudence* has recently been re-issued in paperback.

Films shown during this week are designed to illustrate and extend the Langerian and Adlerian arguments, as well as to serve as test cases for the criteria offered in the preceding session. *Broadway Express, Good Night Socrates,* and excerpts from *Twelve Angry Men* (in the form of the British Film Institute's *The Critic and Twelve Angry Men*) have been used for several years. All three are American, produced within the last decade, and concerned with big cities. To greater or lesser extent each deals with ethnic minorities. All confine themselves to closed worlds: a subway train, the "Greek Town" of Chicago, a jury room. All are within a realistic style. Yet they are very different films, one from the other, in the approach of art to reality. The range is from the least shaped to the most.

THE PSYCHOLOGY OF FILM. The lectures devoted to the psychology of film are divided between social content, with some references to psychoanalytical criticism, and the effects of film on social attitudes, with special attention to the findings of psychophysical psychology.

Starting with the assumption that all art works must in some ways reflect the cultures in which they are created, it is suggested that film and the mass media generally offer especially useful reflective surfaces. Early researchers (e.g., Edgar Dale, *The Content of Motion Pictures,* 1935) found that film portrayed a distorted social reality—that it was fantasy used for escape. Later observers noticed that large chunks of literal social reality nonetheless appear—particularly among those films having some of the intentions or styles of documentary or of social criticism: the "problem pictures." Lewis Jacobs' *The Rise of the American Film* (1939) is used as an example, especially his discussion of the Hollywood themes of the Depression years. More recent is the notion of film content as a complicated manner of dealing with real attitudes and problems cloaked in palatable form—the most significant "message" residing in the underlying assumptions, unintentional and subconscious. Martha Wolfenstein and Nathan Leites' *Movies: A*

Psychological Study (1950) is discussed as illustration. Siegfried Kracauer's *From Caligari to Hitler* is an even more impressive exploration of the ways in which films provide clues to "hidden mental processes," revealing a people's "psychological dispositions," to use his own terms.[1]

Discussion of the effects of film includes the perceptual psychologists' descriptions of the peculiar situation of film viewing, to which can be attributed considerable powers of influence. The primary fact is that movies are shown in the darkest of theaters (with no breaks for intermission) and, with flashing light and shadow, resemble the situation for hypnosis—or sleep, with the dreams provided.

We end with the sociologists' and social psychologists' effects analyses, ably summarized by Joseph T. Klapper in *The Effects of Mass Communication.* One of Klapper's conclusions is that "selective perception" and "selective retention" result in film messages being largely unnoticed, forgotten, or distorted by those originally opposed to the message.[2]

The films shown during this week were all produced to have an effect upon audiences' attitudes and actions. They reflect their times and societies to a useful degree as well. All have to do with war, and each is from a different country and period. *Triumph of the Will* starts us in Nazi Germany in 1934–36—a powerful prefiguration of and contribution toward an impending holocaust. *London Can Take It,* the first widely successful propaganda documentary to come out of beleaguered Britain in the early war years, is remarkable in its contrasts with *Triumph.* Lastly, *Language of Faces,* made fifteen years after that war, is an effort to prevent a next one.

THE TECHNIQUE OF FILM. During the first week of the two-week unit on technique, film is approached as a composite art, collectively created. A day is spent comparing and contrasting it

[1] Princeton, N.J.: Princeton University Press, 1947. Pp. 6–7.
[2] Glencoe, Ill.: The Free Press, 1960. Pp. 21, 23.

with the other arts, particularly those which it most closely resembles and borrows most heavily from: painting and still photography, literature, and drama. Then the multiple skills of film making are traced back to the traditional arts: cinematography (painting and photography), sets (architecture), script (literature), acting (drama), and usually music and sometimes dance. The director as "creator" of the film, the *auteur* theory, is argued.

During this week we see three films with sources in the other arts. The "Diving Sequence" of *Olympia* can be thought of as an extension of still photography into time and motion. *A Time Out of War,* based upon a short story, is a motion-picture equivalent of that literary form. *The Bespoke Overcoat* is close to a filmic record of the Wolf Mankowitz play.

During the second week on the technique of film we drop the comparative approach and consider film as a distinctive visual, narrative, and dramatic art, with its own anatomy. Each aspect is discussed.

Formerly, in talking about the anatomy of film, we mostly reviewed the basic grammar worked out in silent film, from Porter, through Griffith, to Eisenstein, and described in the standard books on film technique and theory. Lately, as I have come to understand a little more clearly the implications of the new styles developing since the mid-fifties (partly the result of changing technology: wide screens, lightweight and extremely flexible cameras and sound recorders), I have been able to contrast the present with the earlier main line.

The films shown during the second week on technique last year were *The Adventurer* (Chaplin, silence, and intricate but pure chase), *Skyscraper* (Shirley Clarke's treatment of the metamorphosis of the 666 Building from hole in the ground to multi-storied completion), and No. 3 of the *Critic and Film Series* (long excerpts from and Basil Wright's brilliant analysis of *Odd Man Out*). All three examples seem to me to represent film's distinctiveness. All are using the medium fully and richly. Yet they represent extremely varied techniques and styles. With *The Adventurer* we talk about what's funny—the characteristics of screen comedy and the elements of Chaplin's conception. *Skyscraper* involves discussion of the suggestions of Broadway (or M.G.M.) musicals which replace traditional documentary sobriety, and what can only be described as Mrs. Clarke's dancer's view of the world. In talking about *Odd Man Out,* Wright stresses its peripatetic structure, explicating and illustrating how all of the aspects (camera, lighting, cutting, sound, performance, even costume) grow out of and fit back into the organizing principle. Further, the sort of textual analysis which he practices offers itself as a model for students in relation to their project films.

THE EXPERIMENTAL FILM. During the eighth week, experiment in the film is dealt with. The point is made that film, as a popular art, is peculiarly vulnerable to technological change brought about by economic pressures and by the inclination of audiences towards an ever more detailed representation of reality. This is largely in contrast to the traditional arts, in which change has been occasioned by aesthetic requirements such as new styles and techniques and, to the extent that this applies, technologies invented to deal with new insights into the human condition. But in film drastic technological-aesthetic modifications have been introduced through financially motivated decisions confirmed by audience acceptance. The "talkies" were born not because creators and critics had been wringing their hands, crying "If only we had sound," but because of the unbalanced ledger of a relatively small firm owned by four brothers named Warner. As a matter of record, creators and critics had to double-time to catch up.

With technologically motivated experiment set forth, it is possible to turn to the experimental film proper. It represents something a little closer to what we mean by the experimental novel, or experimental painting or theater or music. Its development seems to parallel that of the other modern arts, growing as they all do out of new conceptions of the universe and man within it.

Examples of experimental films screened last year were *Le Chien Andalou* (surrealist), *Lines Horizontal* (nonobjective), *Very Nice, Very Nice* (impressionistic-social), *The Tender Game* (lyrical-commercial?), and *N.Y., N.Y.* (impressionistic, abstracted into near nonobjectivity). In response to students' conservatism, some faced with the unconventional for the first time, the Thursday morning discussion revolves around the extent to which the stylistic experimentation was necessary to express the ideas and feelings of the artists. In other words, why didn't they do it like "Gunsmoke" so that everybody could understand?

THE DOCUMENTARY FILM. The unit on documentary, like the one on experimental, is in a way an extension of the two weeks on technique. The first session of this week is devoted to problems of definition, or at least description, of documentaries. Their purposes are discussed as lying somewhere or other between the poles represented by Flaherty ("to discover and reveal"[3]) and Grierson (who wrote about the "creative treatment of actuality"[4] but clearly meant moving and shaking). Then there are the documentary subject matters: social, political, economic themes; real, contemporary situations; groups and classes rather than individuals (or individuals standing for groups and classes)—in short, the actual and/or typical rather than the imagined and exceptional. Methods of organization are the argumentative, expository, descriptive, or narrative, with theme rather than plot emphasized.

Some of the second session is devoted to the "relationships between film and reality, artistic truth and literal fact." This is a large order, philosophically, and discussion proceeds from cross-generic contrasts among documentary, fiction, and experimental films in terms of their ascending order of abstraction from reality as generally perceived. The differences are outlined according to purposes, subject matters, production methods, and resultant styles.

[3] Frances H. Flaherty, *The Odyssey of a Film Maker* (Urbana, Ill.: Beta Phi Mu, 1960), pp. 10–11.

[4] Paul Rotha, *Documentary Film* (New York: Hastings House, 1952), p. 70.

Since examples of all three genres have been screened by this time, we work from the evidence.

As an illustration of documentary, we always see a film which was meant to move and change, and one which involves discovery and revelation. Last year we saw first *The Way Back.* Made to acquaint area residents with the work of the Rehabilitation Institute of Chicago, to enlist their sympathy, participation, or financial contribution, it seems to me a model of its type. The second choice turned out to be less fortunate. *Where Mountains Float* is only barely subtle propaganda by the Danish government on behalf of its stewardship of Greenland. It was interesting on that basis, but not as an example of what Frances Flaherty has described as "the thing in itself, for its own sake." That's what was needed.

THE CHANGING FORM AND FUNCTION OF FILM. The last week is like a mirage on the horizon, promising to accommodate all of the matters omitted, and to bring us up to date. The first lecture is devoted to changing form: wide and deep images and sounds. In it we discuss stereoscopic projection, wide screen, and the accompanying stereophonic and high-fidelity sound. Other theories and possibilities are referred to, including Eisenstein's Dynamic Square[5] and Abel Gance's tryptych screen[6] (variations on both having been in evidence at world's fairs lately).

The second day is devoted to film's changing function. Having replaced popular theater—the traveling and stock companies of the late 1800's and early 1900's—the movies have in turn been replaced by television as the staple popular entertainment. This has been chronicled by Richard MacCann in *Hollywood in Transition.* The final lecture roughly follows MacCann's topics. It covers the fall of the major studios and rise of the independents; the increased importance of international interchange; the mass audience becoming minority audiences; the easing of censorship; and the

[5] Arthur Knight, *The Liveliest Art* (New York: New American Library of World Literature, 1959), pp. 304–5.

[6] *Ibid.,* p. 307.

working out of a *modus vivendi* with television, toll TV still there in the mid-distance.

We end in an attempt to pull all the loose threads together. It is perhaps sufficient to identify the main line: that the film artist in the mid-sixties has developed because of (and at the same time, outside) the prevailing conditions. There is now a system of international distribution and exhibition, however cranky, which can afford a Kurosawa, a Ray, a Bergman, a Resnais, Truffaut and Godard, Fellini, and Antonioni. If there are enough points in the world where a good film can connect with appreciative audiences for long, even repertory runs, film artists as well as entertainers can be supported. That is, a man can create a film more nearly as a writer creates a novel or a painter a painting—individual expression is no longer completely swamped and vitiated by economic requirements. If such a film can now be paid for, as it often can, the artist-film maker can create another. This to me is the dominant current fact, or at least the one with the most exciting potentials, amongst the modes of film communication.

The final showing, therefore, is of a feature-length film representing the possibility of personal statement within the present economy and aesthetic: the art-industry. In the past, Bergman's *Sawdust and Tinsel* (also known as *The Naked Night*) has been shown. It is, I think, among his major achievements, and is a film which, after the initial shock, profits greatly from analysis and criticism; its riches expanding under persistent examination. The level of this last discussion, contrasted with that of the first few weeks, is usually high, more precise, sophisticated, and relevant—the result of a quarter's work.

If students (and teacher) have learned to see films better, they will also better understand the world so brilliantly mirrored in them. If, in addition, they have learned to communicate appreciation and insight through words, the time has been well spent. It may not seem much, especially if such learning happens to be housed within a few blocks of the world's largest helium bubble chamber or an electronic telescope, but it is not so different after all, and much more essential. For film teachers as well as for teachers of the established humanistic disciplines this kind of teaching must always seem enough. Film simply adds itself to a tradition by its presence, by its now unarguable beauty and power in dealing with the concerns of all men.

Supplementary List

Editor's note: The following films were used when "Modes of Film Communication" was offered by Professor Ellis in the Fall Quarter, 1964–65. Addresses of the distributors are found in Appendix A.

Ride the High Country
U.S., 1962, Sam Peckinpah
(Films Inc., 94 min.)

Westinghouse Intro Film
U.S., 1963, Robert Ford
(Westinghouse, 5 min.)

Days to Remember
U.S., 1964, Allan Townsend
(United Charities, 10 min.)

Words, Words, Words
U.S., 1964, G. Hayden Brown
(Northwestern, 20 min.)

Student Engineer
U.S., 1963, Stuart Hagmann
(USIA, 10 min.)

The Homing Pigeon
U.S., 1963, Robert Ford
(Pigeon Racing Assoc., 25 min.)

Assorted Commercials
U.S., 1963–64, various producers
(Chicago TV Stations, 7 min.)

A Dancer's World
U.S., 1957, Peter Glushanok
(Indiana, 31 min.)

Interpretations and Values
U.S., 1958, American Cinema Editors
(A.C.E., 30 min.)

Grassroots
U.S., 1962, Denis Mitchell
(Indiana, 29 min.)

Broadway Express
U.S., 1960, Michael Blackwood
(Contemporary, 18 min.)

Good Night, Socrates
U.S., 1962, Stuart Hagmann and Maria Moraites
(Contemporary, 34 min.)

The Critic and Twelve Angry Men
U.K., 1963, British Film Inst.
(Contemporary, 25 min.)

Triumph of the Will
(abbreviated version)
Germany, 1936, Leni Riefenstahl
(Museum of Modern Art, 40 min.)

A Time Out of War
U.S., 1954, Dennis and Terry Sanders
(Contemporary, 22 min.)

The Bespoke Overcoat
U.K., 1955, Jack Clayton
(Contemporary, 37 min.)

The Adventurer
U.S., 1917, Charles Chaplin
(Contemporary, 20 min.)

Skyscraper
U.S., 1959, Shirley Clarke
(Brandon, 21 min.)

Critic and Film Series, No.—3; Odd Man Out
U.K., c. 1948, British Film Inst.
(Contemporary, 35 min.)

Le Chien Andalou
France, 1929, Luis Bunuel and Salvador Dali
(Museum of Modern Art, 20 min.)

Lines Horizontal
Canada, 1962, Norman McLaren
(Contemporary, 6 min.)

Very Nice, Very Nice
Canada, 1963, Arthur Lipsett
(Contemporary, 8 min.)

The Tender Game
U.S., 1958, John Hubley and Faith Elliott
(Indiana, 6 min.)

N.Y., N.Y.
U.S., 1957, Francis Thompson
(Indiana, 15 min.)

The Way Back
U.S., 1964, Robert Ford
(Rehabilitation Inst. of Chicago, 29 min.)

Where Mountains Float
Denmark, 1954, Bjarne Henning-Jensen
(Brandon, 50 min.)

Hand in the Trap
Argentina, 1961, Leopoldo Torre Nilsson
(Audio, 90 min.)

FILM CRITICISM

by Edward Fischer

IF TEACHING IS AN ART, the teacher like every artist must find his own way of being effective. He dare not copy slavishly any one system, and yet he might study various systems for ideas and inspiration.

The teacher is part of the subject, especially when teaching an art form. He teaches himself—his insights, tastes, and attitudes. He reveals his bias. In teaching an art he reveals himself more completely than he would if he taught such courses as chemistry, accounting, or engineering. Since the individuality of the teacher is so important in the arts, there is a danger that the teacher will make too much of it. His course may be merely a prolonged exercise in personal bias, a parading of the ego. Worst of all it may be formless.

No course should be formless. It is especially ironic if the arts are taught in a formless way, because a regard for form has something to do with a regard for art. The teacher, like the artist, creates by bringing order out of chaos. There is no point in causing unnecessary confusion in a class through a chaotic lack of form. No one would be apt to start a course for beginners in mathematics by teaching calculus the first day, geometry the second, and algebra

---

EDWARD FISCHER is a Professor in the Department of Communication Arts at the University of Notre Dame where he teaches writing, design, and film criticism. In addition to lecturing on film studies both here and abroad, he is the author of *The Screen Arts* and over six hundred magazine articles, and has written and directed documentary films.

the third. Yet this hodge-podge system is sometimes used in teaching the arts.

In the arts a teacher is trying to sensitize students to a certain kind of order. He does this because an aesthetic experience seems to spring from a sensitivity to order. An aesthetic experience is a thrill of the spirit when in the presence of something done with "rightness." I speak of the rightness with which an artist imbues his work, a rightness that reflects unity and order.

So a teacher in film studies ought to arrange his course in such a unified way that the student feels the form of it. The student should sense rightness in the development of the course as a whole and in each class period. Through this repeated experience he becomes more sensitized to the unifying force inherent in a work of art. This preference for the well-wrought object—like a preference for moral goodness—is promoted more through example than through admonition.

The course I shall describe was introduced into the Department of Communication Arts in 1960, is repeated each semester, and is offered for teachers in the summer session. This course is worth three hours of academic credit. Classes are held as two-hour sessions on Monday and Wednesday afternoons. Monday is given over to a lecture and to a discussion of the film that had been screened on the previous Wednesday.

After each Wednesday's screening the students write their observations in from three hundred to five hundred words and turn in their papers by Friday noon. On Monday I tell the students in what areas their papers showed general agreement and the discussion goes on from there.

I have observed that if students write a criticism before the discussion period, the discussion is much more intelligent. The discipline of putting their observations about the film down on paper keeps students from half-saying things and from rambling the way they are apt to do if they merely discuss the film, especially if the discussion follows immediately upon the screening. Written criticism also provides an intellectual discipline that discourages those who are merely looking for a course that requires slight effort.

There is no required reading in this course. However, I do ask students to attend films shown on campus and in town in addition to those they see in class. Before asking the students to write a criticism, I give four lectures and screen a film and discuss that film in some detail. This gives them some idea of what I am looking for, and lessens the frustration and uncertainty that would be theirs if they were asked right away to criticize a film without some orientation.

The first of the four lectures defines terminology and describes film-making technique. Since we need a common terminology for our discussions, I define such terms as scene, sequence, fade, dissolve, and so on. As for film-making technique, I explain to the students that films are often shot out of sequence, in short takes, and some parts are shot over and over. From this mass of exposed film, parts are clipped out and cemented together into what is hoped will be an aesthetic experience.

I explain these things because if the students understand the technique of film making it helps them understand the nature of the medium. By understanding techniques they come to understand how films differ greatly from stage plays. By understanding technique they begin to realize how important the director is and why film editing is an art. They begin to comprehend how directing and editing can create a performance for an actor, and so realize how nonprofessional actors can be effective on screen in a way they could never be on stage.

Understanding technique also helps students develop some aesthetic distance to the performance. In other words it makes students aware not only of the *what* but also of the *how* of a production. One can never be an effective critic without this double awareness.

A good example of aesthetic blindness caused by single awareness was found in pioneer western audiences: some members so completely identified with what happened during melodramas that they threatened to shoot the villain. The unsophisticated audience identifies with what is happening, but fails to be aware of how it is happening, fails to be aware of the art of the thing. An understanding of film-making technique is one of the things that can help develop in students the double awareness of the what and the how.

The second lecture covers visual languages. Since films speak more to the eye than to the ear it is useful, early in the course, to study the alphabet and the grammar of visual language. I teach this by applying to motion pictures the basic principles of design. I try to make the students aware that the very composition on the screen speaks a visual language. A composition that is mainly horizontal is restful, peaceful, soothing. A vertical composition speaks of strength and may even inspire awe. A diagonal composition is dynamic.

The angle from which a camera sees its subject also speaks a visual language. If the camera is down looking up at the subject it makes the subject seem worthy of admiration, or joyful, or victorious. You might call it a positive angle. If the camera is up looking down on the subject it makes the subject seem inferior, depressed, defeated—a negative angle.

The importance of a recurring visual motif is also described in this second lecture. If a visual motif is repeated throughout a film it helps bring visual unity, and if it has significance, as it should, it also makes a statement. For instance, the recurring visual motif in Bergman's *Virgin Spring* is water. We learn in the closing sequence what symbolism Bergman attaches to it, for here he reveals it as a symbol of the redemptive force coursing through the world. In *Citizen Kane,* newspapers recur in many ways, sometimes in happy ways, sometimes in grim ways, depending on the fortunes of Charles Foster Kane, a newspaper tycoon. In *The Set-Up,* clocks recur to give the feeling that time is running out on a prizefighter's career, a career already stretched in defiance of time.

Another thing that I try to help the students see during the second lecture is that the very shape of the motion-picture screen has something to do with the kind of story told and how it is told. The standard screen is close to the proportion that the Greeks called the golden sector. This shape is the one the film director finds most often usable in composing his shot. The long narrow screen confronts the director with a compositional problem and a story problem. I try to help students realize that *Lawrence of Arabia* is an effective film partly because Lawrence's biography lends itself to the long narrow screen in a way that a story such as *Marty* does not. *Lawrence* features the desert, camel caravans, battles—all things that thrive on panoramic display. Yet, if the stage play about Lawrence had been filmed for a panoramic screen it would have made for a restless three hours, for the audience would sense that the medium was not being used effectively.

The third lecture is on the nature of the medium: What seems to fit the motion-picture medium and what seems to abuse it? I explain to the students that each art form has its own way of being effective, its own special glory. Once they understand that they are not so apt to complain that a film wasn't like the book or it wasn't like the play.

Movement and visualization are the two key words in this third lecture. I try to show the students that movement is one of the ways a film has of being effective. A camera cannot only get around from location to location but once it reaches a location it can at each instant give the audience the most effective view through the long shot, medium shot, close up, reverse angle, high angle, low angle. It can isolate inanimate objects or parts of the human anatomy—mouth, eyes, hands—to have them make effective statements when they fill the screen.

I try to make the students aware of the psychology of movement: a movement toward the camera is stronger than one away from it; an upward movement is stronger than a downward movement; a diagonal movement is dynamic; a movement from right to left is more dramatic than one from left to right.

In this third lecture I also explain how editing presents a problem in movement: the very length of the strips of film cemented together causes a rhythm or a lack of it. Long strips cemented together, slow tempo; short strips, fast tempo. This visual tempo needs to change to stay in harmony with the story being told at any given instant.

During the part of this lecture that stresses the visual I explain how the director can draw the audience into the creative process. He gets the audience to participate, for example, through juxtaposition of images on the screen or through subjective camera.

With juxtaposition of images the director says to the audience, in effect, I'll give you two images if you give me a third in return. In *The Music Man,* the director presents the audience with a close-up of several gossips with their heads close together; he cuts to several chickens with their heads close together pecking on the ground. The audience laughs at a third image, the one it creates, the image of old-hennishness.

Through subjective camera the director involves the audience in the creative process by letting it look at the world through the eyes of someone else. At the opening of *Requiem for a Heavyweight* the audience sees the world through the eyes of a defeated prizefighter. It does not see the fighter but sees everything in a stumbling out-of-focus way, in a lurch down the aisle of the arena. It sees the fighter for the first time when he sees himself reflected in the mirror of a cigarette vending machine. He gets a jolt when he sees his battered face and the audience gets a jolt too. The audience's jolt is greater than it would have been had it stood aside and watched the man lurch down the aisle. Having seen the world through his eyes it has had a chance to identify with him.

Anyone criticizing films needs to be made aware of how a director uses outward signs to tell of inward thoughts and emotions. In *The Visit* a snarling panther is sometimes seen looking over a woman's shoulder, and from that visual image the audiences senses the inner woman. In *La Dolce Vita* we see a French actress with a headless statue of Venus behind her, and we know that the actress has a body but not much of a head. In *On the Waterfront* when

Terry tells Edie what he knows of her brother's murder we see a close-up of Edie's face and then a close-up of a steam whistle blowing and we feel the pressures bursting in Edie's spirit. The students soon realize that such cinematic language when used effectively can speak more convincingly than words. Robert Flaherty said something to the effect that film cannot say as much as words but what it can say it can say with more conviction.

In the fourth lecture I speak of the ways the cinema is similar to other art forms.

What is this sense of *rightness* that all artists seem concerned with in every art form? Someone defined an artist as a person who makes things "right." This seems a good definition because artists are always saying the word "right" either aloud or to themselves. An artist may stand before a painting and say, "That upper left-hand area, it's just not right." He may spend a day picking a few notes out on a keyboard trying to get them to fall into a pattern that seems right. He may put a line of poetry on paper and spend the morning rewriting it, trying to get it right.

Is beauty, artistic beauty, a synonym for this rightness? How does the word beauty as used in aesthetics differ from the popular use of the word? To help students understand how far beauty is removed from mere prettiness I screen *A Light for John,* a short film made by a student at the University of Southern California.

John, about thirty years old, is mentally retarded. He lives with his mother, a woman of about sixty. She is the light in John's dim world. The student who made the film tried to show this touching relationship with all the truth that he had the courage to face.

John and his mother play themselves; they are not professional performers. Neither one is pretty. The flat they live in is downright ugly. The calendar art on the wall is ugly. Nothing on the screen is pretty, but the film, as a whole, is beautiful. Beautiful in the sense of being beautifully done. This is artistic beauty and it seems synonymous with truth, integrity, and this rightness that artists are always working for.

I ask the students to imagine a lesser artist using the same subject matter. He might cast a striking actress as the mother and a good-looking young man as John. He might put them in a three hundred dollar a month apartment. Each evening when John comes home from his newspaper stand he might have a martini and count his change under a Picasso. This version would be filled with prettiness but artistically it would be ugly. Through this simple example students begin to comprehend how the homely and the ugly can be artistically beautiful if the artist is capable enough.

If this is the only point that strikes home during the semester the course has not been taught in vain. For most people do not seem to have this discernment. They don't want beauty, they want prettiness. They want to see people on the screen to whom they would like to be related. They want to see apartments they would like to live in. They can't appreciate *A Light for John* because it does not offer the escapism they seek. Instead of giving them a lift of the spirit, a lift that an aesthetic experience gives, it will only annoy and depress them because they do not "get" it. No one prepared them for beauty.

Economy of means is another characteristic desirable in all art forms. This skill in making everything count, in making everything add up, is the touch of the master. It is the opposite of the superfluous, opposite of the excessive.

A good example of economy of means is found in the breakfast table sequence in *Citizen Kane.* In a little more than two minutes we see Charles Foster Kane and his wife grow apart. We first see them as a newly married couple sitting close together at the breakfast table. In a series of brief scenes we see them grow older and speak less as the breakfast table grows longer. In the final scene Kane is at one end and his wife is at the other of a long, long table. He is reading the newspaper he publishes; she is reading the opposition's paper and no words are spoken. In just a short time we are made to believe that we have witnessed something that took years to happen.

I felt frequent frustrations during these first four lectures when

I described scenes as I describe them here. I kept feeling that I should not be describing them in words, either written or spoken, but should be showing them. I felt uneasy using one medium to make points in another.

This particular frustration I was able to do something about. Recently I spent a semester in the studio of OFM Productions, in Los Angeles, adapting the four lectures into four half-hour films. We used demonstrations and film clips to make the points I had been making with the lecture method only.

As I said earlier, after the first four lectures I screen a film and discuss it in detail. For this first film I select one with virtues easily demonstrated such as *Citizen Kane, On the Waterfront,* or *The Set-Up.*

In scheduling films that students will review I find it best to begin with those of universal appeal where the art is quite evident and to move, by degrees, to those that are more sophisticated, that appeal to a more specialized taste.

Toward the beginning of the course I schedule such films as *Treasure of Sierra Madre, I'm All Right Jack, Teresa,* and toward the end, *Seventh Seal, Umberto D, Ikiru.* We screen about fourteen theatrical films a semester. As a transition from theatrical to documentaries I screen theatrical films that show a strong documentary influence—*The Quiet One, Little Fugitive, The Great Adventure.* The last three weeks of the course we screen and discuss such documentaries as *Nanook, The True Glory, Friendship Seven, Thursday's Children, El Puente, Corral;* about fifteen in all.

While screening documentaries I try to help the students see that the best ones are highly factual and yet are imbued with poetic vision. It is such vision that gives meaning to a fact, causes it to glow.

Through poetic vision, *Night Mail,* a British documentary, does more than present facts about the nightly journey of the Postal Special from London to Glasgow. It helps the audience realize that the mail train rushing through the night is not just a silly thing filled with sound and fury, carrying men who futilely sort letters into boxes. Its creators—John Grierson, Basil Wright, Benjamin Britten, and A. W. Auden—make us aware of the dignity of the ordinary because as artists they are aware of the importance of things, even ordinary things. Through poetic vision they help us realize that the men on the train are sorting hopes and fears and that in thousands of homes people await the postman's knock because no man can stand to feel forgotten.

Another British documentary, *Terminus*, says quite a bit to anyone who gets the unspoken message because its facts are given meaning through the poetic vision of the men who made it. It is a candid study of what happens during a day in London's Waterloo Station.

It opens with a man tending beehives on the roof of the station. To anyone who sees this merely as a piece of amusing information and nothing more, it is entertainment but not insight. One must realize that the bees in the hive and the people in the station below are not without similarity. As the day wears on in Waterloo Station the film helps us realize how detached people become when they must deal with great masses. The concern for the individual becomes less, and dehumanization follows in the wake of mass movement.

It is well to lead students to such insights, because the best chance that an individual has of not becoming dehumanized when caught in a complex organism is to be aware of the danger. When a teacher leads students to such realizations, he is much more of a teacher than when he asks them to memorize the twelve rules for something or other. If students see *Terminus* without insight they are just going to learn that there is a railroad station in London that is mighty busy all day long—factual information and nothing more. We are already inundated with too much of such education.

I use *Universe* to show students in what unusual ways a religious film can crop up. No film librarian will ever file *Universe* under Religion, but it is far more religious than many of the films filed under that heading. It won't get under that heading because it lacks religious image and symbol; it makes no special point of being religious. *Universe* tells about the universe with sound, scientific facts. Yet it is much more than the run-of-the-mill astronomy film that lacks inspiration. Just how *Universe* can be so saturated with the glory of God without commenting on it is difficult to discern. Yet, there it is.

Even after students begin writing their observations about films, the Monday lectures continue. As the semester progresses, we discuss such problems as culture and propaganda reflected in films.

If through film studies a teacher leads students to an appreciation of a culture other than their own, he has done something educational. Too many people, even many who have diplomas, think that a culture other than their own ought not exist. This attitude is most evident when they travel abroad resenting everything that is different; they want the whole world paved just like the street they live on.

So often a great director re-creates a culture on the screen only to have the audience resent what he has done, for he has presented a way of life unfamiliar to them. Instead of realizing that here is an opportunity to live beyond what their own living can be, they say, "Down with it!" This is often true of films that honestly explore some aspect of history.

In the film, *The Flowers of Saint Francis,* Rossellini re-created a culture and in so doing left the film open for unpopularity, something it received in abundance. Because the culture of the thirteenth century is unfamiliar it left many people in the audience feeling uneasy, and so they lashed out at the film.

Hollywood's film about Saint Francis was more popular because it superimposed our contemporary culture upon a setting. It left the audience feeling that Francis and Claire were the boy and girl next door, dressed in costume, play-acting. It was easy to imagine that the performers, after a day of shooting, put on sports clothes and roared away to a piazza in a Thunderbird. This was not easy to imagine in the Rossellini film because the cast was so steeped in the Middle Ages that the present seemed far away.

When we take up the problem of propaganda in art, I quote a sentence that Arthur Knight wrote in *The Saturday Review:* "It is the lesser artist, operating from precept rather than perception, who lays himself open to the charge of propaganda."[1]

To demonstrate how propaganda can damage a motion picture I screen two that have great artistic merit, *The River* and *The City,* except for a spot where propaganda is stuck in. It is remarkable how quickly students become adept at detecting the dead spots.

In *The River,* the sequences that show how man blighted this land are wonderful. We see him cut down trees and allow the soil to wash away. Then come the flood sequences, some of the most exciting ever put on a screen. Then the solution: The government must step in and do something. Suddenly the film wilts.

In *The City* the same thing happens. Man blights the city and turns it into a slum. How wonderfully the camera tells this. Then the solution: Move people into planned communities outside of town. Again, banality.

The River and *The City* say the government should do something. *Good Night Socrates,* in telling of the tearing down of Greek Town in Chicago, suggests that when the government meddles in people's lives it causes more wounds than it knows. I like to screen all three of these films the same day, because all three reflect poetic vision and yet they present opposite sides of the fence in their political outlook.

During these screenings I hope to help the students to realize how neutral art is. It can bloom or wilt on any side of the fence. It does not exist to favor a special political bias, or philosophy, or theology, or economic theory, or sociological dream. It is the artist who is on trial. Is he able enough?

Film study is found in two other courses in the Department of Communication Arts. The stress is on aesthetics in the course

[1] "The Art of Meaning," June 6, 1964.

"Modern Culture," and on film making in "Television Production."

Since 1948, "Modern Culture" has offered a survey of contemporary art. Here the students perceive that the cinema blends all other art forms and that it is useful to study all the arts if one is interested in film criticism.

In "Television Production" students make short films in 16-mm. This attempt at film making, like studio work in oil painting, gives a certain insight that theory alone cannot give. A former student of mine, a nun, has her high school class make 8-mm. films because their attempts bring a better appreciation of theatrical films. She says, "I think that making short movies is to full-length features what paragraph writing is to novel analysis. The attempt at creation in the same medium is one of the most direct approaches to appreciation."

Such words as film appreciation and film production may still cause some educators to cringe. For so long they acted as though the arts are mere frivolities. They did not take it for granted that the arts are necessary in developing an educated man.

One reason that educators may have lacked interest in developing discernment and in developing the imagination is that those things are practically impossible to grade. It is not like grading a student on whether or not he has memorized the eight rules for this and the six reasons for that. Something not readily graded, such as discernment and imagination, can be an annoyance and a frustration in a grade-oriented system.

Fortunately more and more educators are becoming interested in the quality of life and not just in the quantity of it. With this interest in quality, the arts, which are essentially life enhancing things, are finding recognition.

The more the arts find a place in education the more film studies will prosper. It is interesting that the cinema should come along and unite the arts in an era that is beginning to yearn for all kinds of unities—ethnic, religious, economic, political.

Since the cinema requires a broad interest in the arts, all of the arts may, in time, be healthier for it. If an English teacher wants to teach film studies he must admit that there is more to communication than the printed word, and if an art teacher wants to become involved with film studies he must show some interest in literary matters. The traditional fragmentation of the arts may become a thing of the past.

More and more educators are admitting that for too long the school catered to the memorizing man while giving scant attention to the feeling man. The talented student whose strong suit was sensitivity, imagination, intuition, was made to feel out of place. With this awareness educators are turning more and more to the arts, seeing them as a way of stretching the boundaries of awareness; seeing them as an insurance against the encroaching vulgarization of life. And, above all, seeing that the arts can bring consolation—the consolation of knowing that man is capable of strong and noble and orderly things even in a disheveled world.

Supplementary List

Following is a list of motion pictures that may be of help to anyone offering a course for beginners in film studies. A key to film distributors follows the listing; addresses are found in Appendix A.

THEATRICAL FILMS

Bad Day at Black Rock U.S., 81 min. (FI)

Ballad of a Soldier (1960) U.S.S.R., 89 min. (AFC)

The Bicycle Thieves (1949) Italian, 87 min. (FC, B)

Boomerang! (1947) U.S., 88 min. (FI, FC)

The Bridge on the River Kwai British, 161 min. (FC, T, AFC)

Brief Encounter British, 99 min. (UWF, CF)

Citizen Kane (1941) U.S., 119 min. (FC, B, CF, FI)

Death of a Salesman (1951) U.S., 111 min. (T, B, AFC, CF, TWF)

The General Line (1929) U.S.S.R., 114 min. (FC)

The Great Adventure Swedish, 75 min. (CF)

Hand in Hand British, 75 min. (T, B, TWF)

High Noon (1952) U.S., 85 min. (FC, T, B, AFC, CF)

The Hustler (1961) U.S., 134 min. (FC, FI)

Ikiru (1952) Japanese, 140 min. (FC, B)

The Informer (1935) U.S., 91 min. (FC, B, CF, FI)

The Island (1961) Japanese, 96 min. (AFC)

La Dolce Vita (1961) Italian, 180 min. (AFC)

La Strada (1954) Italian, 107 min. (FC, B)

The Little Kidnappers (1954) 93 min. (T)

Louisiana Story U.S., 77 min. (CF)

Miracle in Milan (1951) Italian, 95 min. (AFC)

The Mouse That Roared (1959) British, 83 min. (FC, B, AFC, TWF)

The Night of the Iguana (1964) U.S., 117 min. (FC)

Nights of Cabiria Italian, 110 min. (FC, B)

On the Waterfront (1954) U.S., 108 min. (FC, T, B, AFC, CF, TWF)

The Ox-Bow Incident (1943) U.S., 75 min. (FC, B, FI)

Potemkin (1923) U.S.S.R., 67 min. (FC)

The Quiet One (1948) U.S., 67 min. (FC, B, AFC, CF)

The Red Badge of Courage (1951) U.S., 69 min. (FC, B, FI)

Requiem for a Heavyweight U.S., 85 min. (T, B, AFC)

The Set-Up (1949) U.S., 72 min. (FC, MMA, FI)

The Seventh Seal Swedish, 98 min. (J, CF)

The Silent World (1956) French, 86 min. (FC, T, AFC, CF)

The Suitor (1963) French, 83 min. (FC, B)

Teresa (1951) U.S., 105 min. (FC, FI)

The Treasure of Sierra Madre (1948) U.S., 126 min. (FC, T, B, CF, TWF)

The Trial (1962) French-German-Italian, 118 min. (FC, B, CF)

The Virgin Spring Swedish (J)

NONTHEATRICAL FILMS

And Now Miguel (1955) U.S., 63 min. (CF)

Bird Hunt U.S., 15 min. (UC)

The Bulb Changer (1961) U.S., 12 min. (TWF)

The City U.S., 30 min. (CF, MMA)

Corral Canadian, 12 min. (AFC, CF)

Cross-Country Runner U.S., 13½ min. (UC)

Desert Victory British, 62 min. (FC, CF, MMA, TWF)

El Puente (1955) Puerto Rican, 50 min. (MMA)

The Golden Fish (1959) 27 min. (T, AFC)

Good Night Socrates U.S., 34 min. (CF)

Have I Told You Lately that I Love You U.S., 16 min. (USC)

A Light for John U.S., 22 min. (USC)

Moonbird U.S., 10 min. (AFC, CF)

Nanook of the North U.S., 55 min. (FC, AFC, CF, MMA)

Night Mail (1936) British 25 min. (CF, MMA)

Olympia Diving Sequence (1936) German, 5 min. (AFC)

Power Among Men U.S., 45 min. (CF)

The River (1937) U.S., 30 min. (MMA, TWF)

Thursday's Children (1956) British, 22 min. (CF)

Time Out of War (1954) U.S., 22 min. (CF, UC, TWF)

True Glory British, 87 min. (CF, MMA)

Universe Canadian, 28 min. (CF)

FILMS ABOUT FILMS

Critic and Film Series (CF)
1. *Great Expectations,* 6 min.
2. *The Overlanders,* 15 min.
3. *Odd Man Out,* 35 min.

Film Appreciation (1965) U.S., 27½ min. each (OFM)
1. *Elements of the Film*
2. *Film as Visual Language*
3. *Nature of Film Medium*
4. *Film as Art*

Film and Reality British, 105 min. (CF)

You Only Live Once (1937) Excerpts to demonstrate editing, 10 min. (MMA)

Key to Film Distributors

AFC	Audio Film Center
B	Bandon Films, Inc.
CF	Contemporary Films
FC	Film Center, Inc.
FI	Films Incorporated
J	Janus Film Library
MMA	Museum of Modern Art Film Library
OFM	OFM Productions
T	Twyman Films
TWF	Trans-World Films
UC	University of California
USC	University of Southern California
UWF	United World Films

AN APPROACH TO FILM HISTORY

by Arthur Knight

"THE CAMERA," Iris Barry used to say, "is a machine for seeing better with"—to which I would merely add that ever since its invention, creative film makers have been manipulating it to make it see better *their* way. For it is a fundamental of this fascinating and perverse mechanism, that it does not view the world at all the way we do. It cannot perceive true depth, it distorts perspectives and gives false emphasis to whatever is closest to the lens, and at the same time its field is limited—even in Todd-AO's widest "bug-eye" lens—to but a fraction of our normal arc of vision. And yet precisely in these deficiencies lies the basis for all film art. Once the movies' first audiences got over the novelty of seeing shadows move, once movement alone had lost its magic, and the incessant parades, waterfalls, and locomotives of the movies' earliest years failed to produce wonder (or revenue), the film makers had to discover new ways to delight and stimulate the public. Some travelled to the far corners of the earth and brought back scenes that had the appeal of the strange and the exotic; others stayed at home

---

ARTHUR KNIGHT is Adjunct Professor in the Cinema Department of the University of Southern California. He is Curator of the Hollywood Museum, Contributing Editor (film critic) of *The Saturday Review*, author of perhaps the most widely-used book on motion-picture history, *The Liveliest Art*, and a former Assistant Curator of the Museum of Modern Art Film Library.

and invented little stories to put before the camera. For both, however, the problem was essentially the same—to make their pictures look real and feel psychologically true.

The history of motion pictures as an art form is largely a record of the attempts and experiments of gifted men (and all too few women) to make films that were more alive and meaningful, films that had the power to stir the emotions and touch the heart—or even, on occasion, the mind. From Porter to Griffith to Eisenstein, from Clair to Welles to Resnais we can discern the gradual extension of the techniques that make this possible. Each builds on the work of his predecessors. Each adds what he finds necessary to force the myopic camera to give back his own strong personal vision of the world, those special ways of seeing that become the artist's style and "signature." Thus, by tracing the development of this medium through its acknowledged masterpieces and a study of the men who created them, we can follow not only its historical growth, but the evolution of its esthetic as well. In this the film is unique; I can think of no other art form in which one can pinpoint so precisely the contributions of the individual artists, or the historical context of those contributions. The origins of painting, sculpture, and music have been lost in the mists of time. One can only conjecture as to their early development—the impulse behind a cave painting, the scale of the Rhodes' Colossus, the sound of a Roman instrument. In films, however, not only have a great many of the major works survived, but all have been produced within living memory—and generally with a good body of authenticating documentation available.

These are, it seems to me, persuasive reasons for using the historical approach to teach films and film appreciation. Actually, the course which I outline below, based largely on my text, *The Liveliest Art* (published in 1957, revised in 1959), grew out of my years (1950 to 1960) on the staff of the City College of New York's Institute of Film Techniques and (from 1960 to the present) at the Cinema Department of the University of Southern

California. Both institutions have offered extended programs in the technical aspects of film production—photography, editing, sound, and so forth. For students who intend to follow film making as a career, this course serves as both an introduction and a background. Just as, in the other arts, prospective practitioners begin with a thorough grounding in the origins and traditions of their medium before moving on to technique, so also should it be with film. Perhaps even more so, since film is such a costly medium. The editing experiments of Kuleshov, the inceptions in sound of Orson Welles, the controlled use of color in Antonioni's *Red Desert* should be part of the film student's background well before he sets hand to Griswold splicer or Movieola. Certainly, every artist should have the opportunity to make his own mistakes—but need he repeat the mistakes of someone else?

Even more important to me, however, is the growing recognition that film appreciation can—and should—stand in the college curriculum next to similar introductory courses in art or music appreciation (as indeed it now does in the curriculum of U.S.C.). If it is true, as Hollywood apologists often state, that the public gets the kind of films it deserves, then anyone truly interested in the potential of this medium is almost obligated to do everything in his power to upgrade that audience. And what better place to begin than in the universities and colleges, where today more than ever the students are seeing and discussing films with overwhelming seriousness. Certainly, one can say of any art form that the more one brings to it, the more he carries away in terms of appreciation, insight, and enrichment. For the liberal arts student, then, this course affords an opportunity to develop a critical approach to what is perhaps the most pervasive and provocative art form of our time. Not coincidentally, for institutions that do not now have, but may be contemplating, a series of film production classes, a course of this kind becomes a logical growing point, at once stimulating and testing the degree of on-campus enthusiasm for more extended motion-picture studies.

I might mention just in passing—but as an added recommendation for the consideration of university heads as yet undecided about how far they want to go in building a film curriculum—it has been my experience both at C.C.N.Y. and at U.S.C. that many students who have registered for this course out of general interest in their freshman or sophomore year have thereupon decided to make motion pictures their major academic activity, since both institutions offered them this possibility. I would estimate that this held true for approximately a third of the students in every class I have given.

One final word of caution: A film course, even one in film appreciation, is not cheap. Unless a minimum of $300 can be set aside for film rentals each semester, unless there is good 16-mm. projection equipment—and preferably someone apart from the instructor to operate it—such a course should not be given. While some films can always be "promoted," and many communities now have film libraries that turn out prints to legitimate educational institutions either free of charge or for minimal rentals, nevertheless the bulk of the films necessary for such a course must come from distributors—either educational or commercial—whose continued existence is dependent upon their income from rentals. I might also add that a room which can be properly darkened, has reasonably good acoustics, and a projection port so that the machine need not be in the classroom itself can add immeasurably to the students' enjoyment and the teacher's efficiency. This may all seem rudimentary, but I shudder as I recall the number of schools, colleges, museums, and universities where I have had to run films in light-filled rooms, with the sound tracks rendered unintelligible through a combination of noisy projectors and extra-"live" walls. To present a course in film appreciation in this fashion is like teaching music appreciation in a boiler factory. And finally, to think of offering a film course without showing a representative collection of outstanding works is like teaching music appreciation without playing any music!

So, if all this is not too discouraging, what follows is a sixteen-week course in the history and esthetics of motion pictures, detailing the development of the medium as an art form. It may be offered either as a once-a-week three-hour lecture and film session, or as a one-hour lecture plus a two-hour lab session for the film showings. It is best if there can be a question and discussion period immediately following each screening. Recommended as required reading for the course: *The Liveliest Art,* by Arthur Knight, and *The Art of the Film,* by Ernest Lindgren—both currently in print. Supplementary readings may be assigned at the discretion of the instructor. This syllabus includes a number of suggested readings for each session, plus films (with distribution sources) that would be most suitable. It should be added that these sources are as of summer 1965, and subject to change without notice.

It is recommended that the distribution agencies be contacted for current catalogs. Not only do titles appear and disappear almost overnight, but prices vary widely and the same film can often be booked from an alternate source at considerable savings. Furthermore, some distribution firms have branches or depositories that may be located near you; and since the renter of a print pays the postage both ways, this knowledge may also result in a savings. But most important, the catalogs themselves may suggest additional titles that you might want to use either as supplements to, or as replacements for, the films recommended above. I happen to think that complete full-length prints should be studied. For teachers to whom time is a pressing problem however, it is important to note that Sterling-TV has prepared an ever-growing series of condensed versions of the films of the past, adapted for classroom use. These half-hour films, with voice-over narration, may either be rented or purchased outright by a university. For further information: Sterling Educational Films, Inc., 241 E. 34th Street, New York, N.Y. 10016.

1. An Art is Born

Nineteenth-century pre-screen developments: Roget's theory of the persistence of vision (1824) and the simultaneous invention of a photographic process; early animation devices with hand-drawn images give way to efforts to animate photographs; the international development of motion-picture cameras as an aid to science—Muybridge and Marey; the drive toward the projection of an image—Reynaud, Lumière, Edison; international debuts of the motion picture, 1895–96. The esthetic relationship of motion pictures to still photography.

Films: *Biography of a Motion Picture Camera* (Film Images)
The Toy That Grew Up (Film Images)
Origins of the Motion Picture (DuArt Film Labs)
Early Edison Films (M.M.A.F.L.)*
Early Lumière Films (M.M.A.F.L.)
The Photographer (U.S.C.)

Readings: *Magic Shadows,* by Martin Quigley, Jr.
A Million and One Nights, Vol. I, by Terry Ramsaye
Beginnings of the Biograph, by Gordon Hendricks
The Edison Motion Picture Myth, by Gordon Hendricks

2. THE THEATRE SETS THE STAGE

Nineteenth-century theatre, with its increasing accent on realism of setting and melodramatic plot, unwittingly prepared audiences' tastes for precisely what the movies could do better; early staged incidents for camera; Georges Méliès and the dawn of narrative films; Edwin S. Porter introduces discontinuous shooting and parallel editing; early narrative forms and the nickelodeon; the movies' first audiences; rise of the Film d'Art in France; the movies gain respectability.

Films: *Queen Elizabeth* program (M.M.A.F.L.)
Georges Méliès program (M.M.A.F.L.)
Famous Actresses program (M.M.A.F.L.)
Films of Georges Méliès (Indiana U.)
The Great Train Robbery (Contemporary)

* Museum of Modern Art Film Library.

Readings: *Stage to Screen,* by A. Nicholas Vardac
The Rise of the American Film, by Lewis Jacobs, pp. 1–94
A Million and One Nights, by Terry Ramsaye, pp. 322–594
The History of Motion Pictures, by Bardèche and Brasillach, pp. 1–90

3. THE BIRTH OF MODERN FILM TECHNIQUE

Enter D. W. Griffith: The Biograph years—innovations and discoveries, collaboration with "Billy" Bitzer, formation of "the Griffith stock company"; groping toward a new art form through camera placement, editing, and acting; the fruition of Griffith's ideas in *The Birth of a Nation* and *Intolerance.*

Films: *The Mother and the Law* program (M.M.A.F.L.) *
The Birth of a Nation (M.M.A.F.L., Audio Film Classics)
Intolerance (M.M.A.F.L., Audio Film Classics)

Readings: *D. W. Griffith: American Film Master,* by Iris Barry (rev. ed.)
The Rise of the American Film, by Lewis Jacobs, pp. 95–119, 171–201
The Movies in the Age of Innocence, by Edward Wagenknecht, pp. 78–137

4. THE MOVIES BECOME BIG BUSINESS

From two-reelers to features; Carl Laemmle leads the fight against the Film Trust; the rise of the star system; the shift from working-class nickelodeons to middle-class entertainment palaces, and its effect upon films; Thomas H. Ince introduces the "unit system" of production; the fight for theater control; the effects of World War I on American films; the rise of Hollywood; million dollar contracts and the formation of United Artists.

* Museum of Modern Art Film Library.

Films: *A Fool There Was* program (M.M.A.F.L.)*
Civilization program (M.M.A.F.L.)
Tol'able David program (M.M.A.F.L.)
Broken Blossoms (M.M.A.F.L., Audio Film Classics)
When the Clouds Roll By program (M.M.A.F.L.)
Way Down East (M.M.A.F.L.)

Readings: *A History of the Movies,* by Benjamin B. Hampton, pp. 64–251
The Movies in the Age of Innocence, by Edward Wagenknecht, pp. 138–219
Douglas Fairbanks: The Making of a Screen Character, by Alistair Cooke
The Rise of the American Film, by Lewis Jacobs, pp. 159–301
The Best Remaining Seats, by Ben M. Hall, pp. 1–68
The Lion's Share, by Bosley Crowther
A Million and One Nights, by Terry Ramsaye, pp. 523–789

5. THE MOVING CAMERA

Background of the film in Germany; *The Cabinet of Dr. Caligari* introduces a subjective use of the camera; the influence of Carl Mayer; the rise of Ufa, Pommer, and big studio production techniques; Murnau introduces the moving camera as a "first person" observer; G. W. Pabst and the psychological placement of the camera; Pabst's editing on movement technique; the "Germanization" of Hollywood in the late twenties.

Films: *The Cabinet of Dr. Caligari* (M.M.A.F.L., Contemporary)
The Last Laugh (M.M.A.F.L.)
Siegfried (M.M.A.F.L., Brandon)
Variety (M.M.A.F.L.)
Secrets of a Soul (Brandon)

* Museum of Modern Art Film Library.

The Love of Jeanne Ney (M.M.A.F.L.,* Brandon)
Metropolis (M.M.A.F.L., Brandon)
The Woman in the Moon (Brandon)

Readings: *From Caligari to Hitler,* by Siegfried Kracauer
The Film Till Now, by Paul Rotha, pp. 252–92, 709–18
The History of Motion Pictures, by Bardèche and Brasillach, pp. 187–95, 251–62

6. EDITING THE IMAGE

Background of the film in Russia; experiments in editing begin with Dziga Vertov and the "Kino Eye" group; the impact of Kuleshov's workshop and its experiments; the contrasting theories of Eisenstein and Pudovkin; the film poems of Dovzhenko; the "new realism" of the Soviet films of the late twenties, and their impact on the Western world.

Films: *Potemkin* program (M.M.A.F.L.)
By the Law program (M.M.A.F.L.)
Ten Days That Shook the World (M.M.A.F.L.)
Mother program (M.M.A.F.L.)
Arsenal (M.M.A.F.L., Brandon)
Earth (Brandon)

Readings: *Kino,* by Jay Leyda
Sergei M. Eisenstein, by Marie Seton
Film Sense and *Film Form,* by Sergei M. Eisenstein
Film Technique & Film Acting, by V. I. Pudovkin
The Technique of Film Editing, by Karel Reisz, pp. 13–40
The Film Till Now, by Paul Rotha, pp. 217–51

7. THE END OF THE SILENT ERA

Toward an international art—the free interchange of films and film artists; penetration of American film into European markets and of European artists into American studios; the rise of film

* Museum of Modern Art Film Library.

societies and art theaters for the specialized audience; the first European *avant garde;* summary of the characteristics of the art of the silent film.

Films: *The Passion of Joan of Arc* (M.M.A.F.L.)*
Seventh Heaven (M.M.A.F.L.)
Sunrise (M.M.A.F.L.)
The Smiling Madame Beudet program (M.M.A.F.L.)
The Italian Straw Hat (M.M.A.F.L.)
Hotel Imperial (M.M.A.F.L.)

Readings: *Reflections on the Cinema,* by René Clair
Theory of the Film, by Béla Balasz
Let's Go to the Movies, by Iris Barry
The History of Motion Pictures, by Bardèche and Brasillach, pp. 223–302
A History of the Movies, by Benjamin B. Hampton, pp. 304–61

8. THE COMING OF SOUND

Early (pre-1900) attempts at sound films; the not-so-silent "silent" films; the work of Lee De Forest; Warner Brothers introduce the Vitaphone; the impact of *The Jazz Singer;* rivalry with Fox's sound-on-film Movietone process; the rush for sound; early dominance of sound technicians in the studios; effects of sound on writers, actors, and directors; the efforts of creative directors—Lubitsch, Clair, Hitchcock, and others—to cope with the new medium.

Films: *The Movies Learn to Talk* (Prudential Ins.)
Sound Recording and Reproduction (Encyclopaedia Britannica Films)
The Coming of Sound program (M.M.A.F.L.)
Singin' in the Rain (Films, Inc.)
Anna Christie (Films, Inc.)
The Jazz Singer (Brandon)

* Museum of Modern Art Film Library.

All Quiet on the Western Front (United World)
The Love Parade (M.M.A.F.L.)*
Sous les Toits de Paris (Brandon)
Blackmail (M.M.A.F.L.)
Hallelujah! (Films, Inc.)

Readings: *Okay For Sound,* by Frederic M. Thrasher
Talking Pictures, by Barret C. Kiesling
Film Daily Yearbook, 1929: "The Onrush of Sound," by Charles F. Hynes, pp. 484–503
A Tree is a Tree, by King Vidor, pp. 159–229
An Hour With the Movies and the Talkies, by Gilbert Seldes
Film as Art, by Rudolf Arnheim, pp. 199–230
Upton Sinclair Presents William Fox, by Upton Sinclair

9. Exploring the Sound Medium

Early dominance of "canned theatre"; technical problems and limitations of early sound films; the new nationalism imposed by sound; René Clair, V. I. Pudovkin, and the principle of "asynchronous sound"; Hitchcock's use of sound montages; the liberation of the medium.

Films: *Le Million* (M.M.A.F.L.)
A Nous La Liberté (Contemporary)
The 39 Steps (United World)
The Public Enemy (Brandon, Contemporary)
The Man I Killed (M.M.A.F.L.)
Trouble in Paradise (M.M.A.F.L.)

Readings: *A Grammar of the Film,* by Raymond Spottiswoode
Film as Art, by Rudolf Arnheim, pp. 8–187
Film Acting, by V. I. Pudovkin
Fun in a Chinese Laundry, by Joseph von Sternberg

10. Toward Integration and Style

New problems posed by sound—editing, handling the actor, the

* Museum of Modern Art Film Library.

development of a cinematic dialogue, music; gangster films and musicals, plus the realistic tendency of the times, help break the theatrical tradition; the writer-director combinations begin to discover a balance; Hollywood in the thirties.

Films: *The Informer* (Brandon, Contemporary, Films, Inc.)
It Happened One Night (Royal 16 Intl.)
Mr. Deeds Goes to Town (Royal 16 Intl.)
Shall We Dance? (M.M.A.F.L.)*
The Grapes of Wrath (M.M.A.F.L., Films, Inc.)

Readings: *Footnotes to the Film,* ed. by Charles Davy
We Make the Movies, ed. by Nancy Naumburg
Film and Theatre, by Allardyce Nicoll
Introduction to the Art of the Movies, ed. by Lewis Jacobs, pp. 163–238
Hollywood: The Movie Colony, the Movie Makers, by Leo Rosten

11. THE CREATIVE SOUND TRACK

The contributions of Orson Welles, based on his training in radio and theater; influences of the radio—use of the narrator, musical bridges, voice and sound montages; the "natural" use of sound, sound perspective, and voice overlaps; collaboration with Gregg Toland, and use of the wide-angle lens for greater photographic clarity and depth.

Films: *Citizen Kane* (Brandon, Contemporary)
The Magnificent Ambersons (Brandon, Contemporary)

Readings: *Orson Welles,* by Roy Alexander Fowler
The Fabulous Orson Welles, by Peter Noble
The Cinema of Orson Welles, by Peter Bogdonovich
Theory of Film, by Siegfried Kracauer, pp. 102–56

* Museum of Modern Art Film Library.

12. THE RESURGENT POSTWAR CINEMA

Heightened film activity in Europe after World War II; developments in England, France, and Italy related to national consciousness kindled by war and its aftermath; Italian neorealism —a technique to match a philosophy; the importance of film festivals.

Films: *Open City* (Brandon, Contemporary)
The Bicycle Thieves (Brandon)
Brief Encounter (United World)
Odd Man Out (United World, Contemporary)
Children of Paradise (Contemporary)
I Vitelloni (Contemporary)

Readings: *The Italian Cinema,* by Vernon Jarratt
French Film, by Georges Sadoul
The Film in France, by Roy Fowler
Scandinavian Film, by Forsyth Hardy
The Contemporary Cinema, by Penelope Houston

13. THE INDEPENDENT FILM ARTIST

The nature of the film collective; re-emergence of a personal style and vision on the screen—Bergman, de Sica, Fellini, Kurosawa, Ray, Rossellini, and others; relation of personal to national styles of film making; government subsidy as a spur to European production; implications of the development of art theaters in the United States.

Films: *Wild Strawberries* (Janus)
The Seventh Seal (Janus)
The World of Apu (Brandon)
Ikiru (Brandon)
Jules and Jim (Janus)
L'Aventura (Janus)
Last Year at Marienbad (Audio Film Classics)
8½ (Embassy 16-mm. Dept.)
Rashomon (Audio Film Classics)
Two Women (Audio Film Classics)

Readings: *The Personal Vision of Ingmar Bergman,* by Jörn Donner
Four Screenplays, by Ingmar Bergman
The Japanese Film, by Joseph Anderson and Donald Ritchie
Indian Film, by Erik Barnouw and S. Krishnaswamy
The Two Hundred Days of 8½, by Deena Boyer
Michelangelo Antonioni, by Pierre Leprohon
Cinema Eye, Cinema Ear, by John Russell Taylor

14. THE INDEPENDENT IN AMERICA

The United Artists revolution, 1950–60; emergence of the corporate star or director as independent producers; effects of television competition—wider screens and the "new maturity"; new directions for American cinema explored by New York "underground" and *cinéma vérité* groups; effects of international competition on current American film production; the emerging specialized audience for films.

Films: *Dr. Strangelove* (Royal 16 Intl.)
David and Lisa (Continental 16)
Beat the Devil (Royal 16 Intl.)
Hallelujah the Hills (Janus)
The Bridge on the River Kwai (Trans-World)
The Most (Janus)
The Savage Eye (Brandon)

Readings: *Hollywood in Transition,* by Richard Dyer MacCann
I Lost It at the Movies, by Pauline Kael
Film: Book 1, ed. by Robert Hughes
The Dreams and the Dreamers, by Hollis Alpert
Anatomy of a Motion Picture, by Richard Griffith

15. THE DOCUMENTARY FILM

Definitions by Grierson and Rotha; the rise of documentary in England, Germany, and the United States; the special role of Robert Flaherty; social content of the thirties; influence on fact films of World War II; postwar influences and decline; resurgence of documentary through television.

Films: *Shipyard* (Cinema 16)
Granton Trawler (M.M.A.F.L.)*
The Song of Ceylon (M.M.A.F.L., Brandon)
Housing Problems (M.M.A.F.L.)
Night Mail (M.M.A.F.L., Brandon)
The City (M.M.A.F.L.)
The River (M.M.A.F.L., Brandon)
The Battle of San Pietro (M.M.A.F.L. or U.S. Signal Corps)
Triumph of the Will (M.M.A.F.L., Audio Film Classics)
Man of Aran (Contemporary)
Louisiana Story (Contemporary)
Episodes from *The Twentieth Century* (Prudential Ins.)
Episodes from *CBS Reports* (McGraw-Hill)

Readings: *Documentary Film,* by Paul Rotha
Grierson on Documentary, ed. by Forsyth Hardy
The World of Robert Flaherty, by Richard Griffith
Films Beget Films, by Jay Leyda

16. The New Avant Garde

The discovery of film as an art form by colleges and universities; influence of low-cost 16-mm. equipment as an incentive toward personal expression in film; the proselytizing of Maya Deren; the rise of Cinema 16, and the film society movement as a spur to young film makers; the world-wide resurgence of experimental film making and its significances.

Films: *Films of Maya Deren* (Cinema 16)
Films of Kenneth Anger (Cinema 16, Film-Makers Cooperative)

* Museum of Modern Art Film Library.

Films of Stan Brakhage (Cinema 16, Film-Makers Cooperative)
Films of James Broughton (Film Images)
Films of Curtis Harrington (Brandon)
Films of Bruce Connor (Creative Film Society)
Films of Stan Vanderbeek (Cinema 16, Film-Makers Cooperative)
Films of Norman McLaren (Contemporary)
Films of James Davis (Film Images)
Films of Ian Hugo (Film Images)
Films of Andy Warhol (Film-Makers Cooperative)

Readings: *Art in Cinema,* ed. by Frank Staffacher
Experiment in the Film, ed. by Roger Manvell
An Anagram of Ideas on Art, Form and Film, by Maya Deren
The Three Faces of the Film, by Parker Tyler
Cocteau on the Film, by Jean Cocteau

FILM AESTHETICS

by Hugh Gray

THE ULTIMATE CONCERN of all of those who deal with the subject of motion pictures in a university setting, is to determine the most effective and imaginative way of fostering their practice and study, as part of a legitimate university or academic concern and as a particular manifestation of man's continuous psychosocial evolutionary transition.

My immediate and personal concern, inside that broad framework, is with the area of aesthetics.

Now it is common knowledge that the whole area of aesthetics is a sensitive one, and none is more sensitive than that area which one might call "kine-aesthetics." It is full of pitfalls, illuminated all too often only by an illusion—creating *ignis fatuus.* Frequently too, while searching through the realm for what Pindar describes as the *thaumaton odon* (the miracle mile?) leading to understanding, the travellers develop an *odium* far out-rancouring the old, original *odium theologicum.* There are some, for example, who, on serious philosophical grounds, deny or refuse the existence of such a subject. These are joined, doubtlessly to their embarrassment, by a group constituted on the one hand by those who suffer from a kind of inverted intellectual snobbery, reaching at times

---

HUGH GRAY is Professor of Theatre Arts at the University of California, Los Angeles. He received his education at the University of Oxford (modern languages) and the Sorbonne (aesthetics and history of art). He has been a film and drama critic as well as a screen writer in England and the United States.

almost pathological proportions, and on the other by the commodity peddlers, who all loudly proclaim that "aesthetics" is for the birds. To these we say in all sweet reasonableness, after the example of Plato, "We will bow down before you and worship you and annoint you and garland you but we must warn you that we cannot have such as you in our republic."

The government, if such existed, that would expel these people could as yet claim only provisional authority, and it is on such a basis that the film aesthetician must proceed.

In other words, in this area one must walk cautiously, humbly, experimentally, and expecting for the moment no more than tentative conclusions. On the other hand one must be buoyed up with the "feeling," the "sense," the hunch, if you like, that there is indeed something there.

It is in this attitude of mind that I offer you my reflections which, in the circumstances can only be personal—personal to one whose assignment it is to conduct a graduate seminar in film aesthetics as part of the curriculum of theater arts on the campus of the University of California, Los Angeles.

The Course

In preparing the course I was faced with a number of questions. The first was one of definition. What is meant by the word "film"? This is the perennially unanswered and perhaps unanswerable question, except perhaps in some very wide, general terms, such as I used at the opening of this paper.

The most common definition might be set out as follows:

A film is something created for the screen with the aid (above and beyond the basic cinematic equipment) of devices; some being proper to film (i.e., editing, camera angles, special effects, etc.), others pressed into service from other arts, primarily theater, painting, and music (i.e., acting, dramatic structure, visual composition, emotional highlighting) for the purpose of recording a story geared to the maximum entertainment of the maximum number.

This definition is not, as too many of those both inside and outside the U.S. would have it, simply a literate rendering of a formula concocted by a group of illiterate tycoons for purely mercenary reasons. It is an aspect of the "down to earth," foursquare, Euclidian attitude toward life, art, and "reality" of the second largest bourgeois society in the West. The first is, of course, the Soviet Union which, ironically, has made of its proletariat a "cultural bourgeoisie"—thus revealing that socialist realism and capitalist realism, in the arts, have much in common. In proof of this, one has only to compare the tastes of the late L. B. Mayer and Joseph Stalin or of Khrushchev and General Eisenhower.

For others including myself, film is not, in *priority of concept,* a story-telling device so much as a language—all culture is by way of language, says the eminent French anthropologist Lévi-Strauss. It is the surrealist medium par excellence. In its essence and nature it is to be distinguished from theater, and it is frequently and inceasingly at its most powerful outside the limits of the structure of the "well-made play," within which the studios have tended to confine it. Above all, I see no reason why, in deliberate intention, each film should be for everybody in any other sense than that in which the man of genius or great talent, setting forth his own concept in his own way, is found to be speaking to and for all mankind and in due course becomes a classic.

A search for an answer to the question, "What is film?" while not ignoring the *practical searching* of film makers from Méliès and Griffith to Bresson and Bunuel, and of the new realists and the new wave, includes the *theoretical speculations* that began with Canudo and were subsequently pursued by Jean Epstein, Gance, and Cocteau, among Frenchmen; by the Italians and the Russians; by the Germans; and by the English documentarians. Today, at last, we have the first formal book of film aesthetics, *L'Esthètique et Psychologie du Cinéma* by Jean Mitry.

The interplay between this *thinking* and the *practice* of film making has over the years added a richness, a flexibility, and a range to the cinema in Europe and elsewhere that has been denied it in the Hollywood studios (as in Moscow since the disgrace of Eisenstein), but which is now finding its way into the film making of the individual and independent young American director whose creative talent, grown impatient with and even contemptuous of the studio formula, promises a new future. The richness of this promise is increasingly evident in the films now being made on some of our campuses.

As to aesthetics, there is a tendency to use the word in a general and loose way as if it referred only to techniques, to the way you get your effects, with a vague sense of something to do with beauty somewhere in the background, mostly felt to relate to photography.

For my own part, I would hazard the following definition: A study, in the light of its causes, of the nature and impact of the perception of a work of art as a work of art (in this case of a film) on our sensitive and cognitive faculties.

Aim and Organization

Our aim is to study the motion picture as a work of art produced by cinematic skills, valued for what it is in itself, and definable as a series or sequence of images, image-forming shadows and sounds, unfolding rhythmically, in time, onto a screen by means of light projected through celluloid, and forming a patterned whole whose existence is truly constituted for the cognitive faculties at the moment of its being perceived in its entirety by the eye (visuals) and by the ear (sounds).

We should note here that this definition would be modified in at least one respect, by the Marxist for whom art is an ideology, that is, a weapon in the class struggle. For him, it would read "an object produced by cinematic skills, to serve as a weapon in the class struggle, and definable as . . . etc."

Taking the unmodified definition as our point of departure, our concern is then with the following:

1. *All that is involved in the process of that specific form of perception;* i.e.:
   a) With the *act of perception* itself.
   b) With the *image* as the instrument of that perception.
   c) With the objective, cognitive *validity* of that image.
   d) With, in elaboration of the foregoing, the question of *reality and realism* to be considered under three aspects.
      (1) *In general,* that is to say, within the framework of an overall concept of "reality." We do well to remember that "if the reason in things is the same as the reason which we acknowledge as the standard of valid thinking about any object, this is only because we ourselves have preordained what conditions any object must meet if it is to be counted by us as real." In short, it is the thinking subject himself who establishes the standards of objectivity. If the world is not, as Schopenhauer misleadingly put it, "my idea," it is at any rate real for us only to the extent that it conforms to our concept of what any real thing must be.
      (2) *In particular,* namely in relation specifically to cinema. Here we do well to call to mind what has been noted by Marcel Martin, among others (*Le Language Cinématographique*): "The reality set forth in the image, is the outcome of selection and composition, that is to say, it is the manifestation of the director's own subjective perception of the world. The cinema offers us an artistic image of reality. In other words, if we reflect upon it, it offers us an "unreal" image (take for example the close-up or the use of music), i.e., a *reconstruction* of reality conforming with what the director wishes to express, both sensuously and intellectually."

(3) *Historically.* The history of the film shows that from the day of its discovery there has been a preoccupation with its relation to "reality." "It's life itself!" "It is nature captured alive!" the pioneers exclaimed, on seeing the results of their first efforts. That was nearly a century ago. Only the other day a television commercial advertising film stock for home movies, used as its slogan, "the film is the nearest thing to life itself!" forgetting to add, "and yet, what worlds away!" All major schools of film making can, in fact, be subsumed under various qualifications of the term "realism."

(*a*) Surrealism.
(*b*) Documentary realism.
(*c*) Socialist realism.
(*d*) Neo-realism (Zavattini speaks of the "cry of reality"[1]).

Again, a major preoccupation of Resnais, one of the "nouvelle vague" directors, notably in *Hiroshima* and *Marienbad,* is with an important human aspect of the problem of reality. This is the continuity (and reality) of the individual, the "self"—man's personal identity. Indeed, the concern of the all-pervasive existentialism of the French cinema is with the *objet,* the *pour soi,* the establishment of the self as a "reality." In this context one might recall the line of the man in the bistro (ironically enough unidentified!) in *Jules et Jim,* who introduces the girl beside him as "*ma femme, objet.*"

e) With *mimesis* as it applies to the motion picture, to which it has a special kind of application. It might be reasonably argued that its application to the motion picture gives us a truer understanding of what Aristotle meant than its application to any other art. For Aristotle *mimesis* means

[1]Robert Hughes (ed.), *Film: Book 1* (New York: Grove Press, Inc., 1959), p. 128.

"imitation of nature as a creative force" and not in a pantomimic or photographic sense. *It is precisely by denying the purely photographic or purely mechanically reproductive function of the movie camera* that the motion picture can be reckoned an art, as Arnheim was, I think, the first to point out.

The conclusions reached from the concept of *mimesis* as applied to the motion picture will of course be tempered and shaped by the conclusions reached concerning the image in section *d*) above. On the other hand, they will not be complete without some reference to the place and role of *things* in cinema. The Russians, among others, have had much to say on this subject, while more recently Sartre and Bazin have made an interesting contribution to it. Both speak of it in terms of the relative role of "man" and "the decor"; the movement, in cinema, being from the decor to man. Bazin goes on to draw attention to a list of directors who give priority of place to things.

f) With the film as *objectivized dream*. Here it is Cocteau who has made a comment that serves us well as a point of departure. "Long live the young muse cinema who is privy to the mystery that is a dream. She it is who allows us to give the shape of reality to the unreal!"

2. *The reactions of the perceiving subject,* that is to say with:

a) *Tragic pleasure.* Here we take a valuable idea from Aristotle's *Poetics* in which was foreshadowed the concept of "aesthetics." We use the notion implied in this term (and by analogy the term "comic pleasure") as the point of departure for an examination of the transforming effect of all that is implied by cinematic form, that is to say, the creative use of all the potentialities of the instrument upon such predisposed primary material as is patient of transformation solely into cinema.

We are without a really adequate word to express the

result. Dramatic does not do. Etymologically justifiable, had cinema come first, it is now too closely associated with theater and with exhibitions of over-emotional behavior. What we are in search of then is an adequate term (cinematic is also pre-empted) conveying jointly the sense of the thing done (*dramata*) with its being *cinematically* done. In other words, we wish to describe the emergence of what is done for the camera and microphone in the very broadest sense ("set-up" might be the word), whether it is by a person, a landscape, or a thing, and which emerges as quite other than as a pure reproduction.

Whatever the term may turn out to be (*cine-mimesis* may serve our purpose), it should suggest that cinema is in fact a special case of man's narcissistic concern with himself and with the human condition, all his emotions before the screen being conditioned forms of this self-recognition. Nor is the term "narcissistic" here used in any pejorative sense. From this it will follow that the concomitant state, namely recreation, lies in the inescapable *re-creation* or repetition or permutation of this indefinitely variable confrontation—a conclusion which leads us naturally to:

b) The concept of *entertainment.* Here we discuss the popular use of this term and of the term "escape," in this context. In the process we try to estimate the true significance of these terms and their relation to the "aesthetic." It is, again, a sensitive area on which, as a rule, there is shed more heat than light. The studios are particularly sensitive to that question, on economic grounds, and have rung over the years with such slogans as "Messages are for Western Union!" or "Satire closes on Friday!" Production personnel, usually the screen writers, with ideas beyond the multiple variants of the "formula," are apt to be viewed with suspicion.

c) *The attitude of the spectator.* The questions here raised are multiple, and their proper study belongs in any depth to other disciplines. Two areas however call for our particular attention.

(1) *Psycho-physiological.* Here we consider the mind of the percipient who is said to be in a state of passivity bordering on hypnosis while watching a film. Attention was first drawn to this subject by Cohen-Séat who founded the Institut de Filmologie at the Sorbonne. More recently investigations have continued at Milan in the Instituto *Agostino Gemelli.*

An excellent example of such studies is to be found in a discussion of the particular process of *alienation* (ex-stasis or identification) created by watching a film. The author of *Introduction to the Findings of the Institute of Milan* (1964) says:

> The mind of the spectator watching a film show, sinks into a sort of dimmed twilight in which neither the conscious nor the unconscious are uppermost, but both are present, simultaneous and joined. The alertness that typifies objective relations in ordinary life is reduced—it may be dimmed to a greater or lesser degree—but it is always brought down to a point where the exercise of the rational critical faculty is less efficient, and the spectator is exposed to traumatic stimuli because the normal defense mechanisms fail to come into action.[2]

What are the effects, aesthetically, of this? What are the consequences in general on the mental and social functioning of the spectators? These are questions which lead us to our second consideration under this heading.

(2) *Mass culture.* This is an area where sociology meets with the aesthetic. It is a problem raised by the exis-

[2] P. 28.

tence and function of the "mass media," and one increasingly to be studied, notably in the light of McLuhan's *Understanding Media.*

d) *The vexed question of beauty,* and the still more vexed question of ugliness:

(1) *Beauty in general.* For this we go back to Plotinus, the neo-Platonist, whose concern it first was, and for a discussion of ugliness we return, say, to Augustine of Hippo. Nor can we forget Aristotle and the Scholastics and their description of beauty, or what Plato had called a divine effulgence and, what all have called "harmony of parts." How objective is it? How subjective? Shakespeare spoke of it as "the eye of the beholder."

And ugliness? Do we approach it as paralleling the Hellenic concept of evil as an absence of order and harmony, or rather as something positive, thereby paralleling the Manichean concept?

(2) *Film and beauty.* The first question that arises is how the concept of beauty at which we may have arrived can be applied in speaking of film. This in turn is part of the question concerning its application to all the arts.

Is beauty, as the formal logicians have it, to be predicted *univocally* of all the arts or by *analogy?* In our attempt to answer this question we have not been well served by the philosophers and historians of art. They speak of the beautiful in relation to the various arts; they list them of course, almost always including theater and only rarely the cinema, and then proceed to discuss beauty in relation only to the plastic arts. Even music is rarely treated. By way of filling that gap I think one might say, as the expression of a reasonably orthodox attitude, that beauty in a film, though in a measure constituted by the single frame or sequence, is not to be sought there, but in the whole—in a complex of harmonies of sight and sound, of gesture and voice, and of a two-fold, interwoven rhythm of action and of montage. Thus a film has so many ways to be "beautiful" and so many to fall short of it.

In this context may I confess that I am continually haunted by that epithet of the Athenians, the *kalon-kagathon* expressing two interrelated aspects, as it were, of one quality in a subject. Maybe in the absence of such a concept from our thinking, something of deep value that was experienced by the Athenian conjointly perceiving the good and the beautiful, is missing from our perception of a work of art.

Certainly, since the eighteenth century and notably since Kant's *Critique of Judgment,* the gap has been widened between the art object and any purpose or function outside it. Some, as we know, have even gone further and speak of art for art's sake. If you had used such an expression in talking to an Athenian he would not have understood what you were talking about.

ANALYSIS OF FILMS. Obviously an important part of our procedure is the analysis of films. This we do by studying them in the light of our definition of aesthetics, with particular reference to:

1. The techniques and methods that produce the "aesthetic effect."
2. Style, examining it as it is exemplified in the words of various outstanding directors.
3. The problem of authorship arising out of considerations of style and aesthetic unity.

COMPARATIVE STUDY OF THE ART OF FILM WITH OTHER ARTS. Although an ingenious attempt was made in a recent article in the British Architectural Review to draw a very close parallel between film and architecture, the usual inter-arts comparison is between film and:

1. *The "spatial art" of painting.* Our chief concern here is with the work of the camera, notably with composition, although there can also be an interesting comparison with tapestry.
2. *The "temporal art" of music.* Here the consideration is with (*a*) structure, (*b*) rhythm, and (*c*) the use of music to give a new dimension to a scene and to heighten emotion.
3. *The "dramatic art" of theater.* This, the most close of the comparisons, we examine:
   a) *In the light of history.* There is, of course, no intrinsic relationship between theater and camera. Historically, however, the association was made quite early, by Méliès. This association leading to the *film d'art,* to the "Famous Players" concept of Lasky is examined in the light of their artistic and, equally important, of their economic reasons.
   b) *In the light of the reaction against filmed theater.* Here we analyze the thinking of Canudo (and his innovatingly fruitful question: what is cinema?) and of those who have followed him, both directors and theorists, in France, Russia, Sweden, Germany, Italy, England, and the U.S. down to the present time. It was in this period of early questioning by men such as Canudo, that "film aesthetics" took its rise, and the essential distinction between theater and cinema was increasingly established. Following on this distinction we go on to examine film in the light of the comparison between what we call:
   c) *The shadow and the substance.* Cinema has been called by one French author, *l'art de l'absence.* It is this condition that brings us to the heart of the distinction between film and theater.

The *locus classicus* is in the confrontation of Henry Gouhier (*L'Essence du Théâtre*) and André Bazin ("Qu'-est-ce que le Cinéma?" Vol. II. *Théâtre et Cinéma*), with Bazin's ingenious answer to Gouhier's definition of the essence of theater as "the real presence of the actor."[3] Bazin's answer (I find it more *ben brovato* than convincing) is that the imprint of the "object" on the "celluloid" is a "reality in nature"; that the "close-up" by virtue of the intensity of its impact, is to all intents and purposes the equivalent of the "real presence" of the actor; that films like *Henry V* and *Les Enfants Terribles* show that cinema can give us theater.[4]

Some Fruits and New Frontiers

All our studies must be carried out with the future of our society in mind, and none more so than cinema in the light of the present and future importance, in so many areas, of this mass medium.

Now the future of our society, of civilization itself, depends in a large measure on the recognition that the old quarrel between the scientist and the poet, between action and contemplation, is a false one and can indeed be fatal. It is interesting to note that it is the scientists who have been first to recognize this. The names of Bronowski and even of Lord Snow come at once to mind. The long revolution has, in some respects, come full circle. Automation and the fruits of the labors of the active Protestant, renaissance man will once more bring twentieth-century man back to a measure of the "contemplative life," condemned at the Reformation as the idle indulgence of fat and lazy monks. Aesthetics belongs to this newly returning contemplative life that brings to man an enrichment of "being" and a guide and support in the final and most challenging confrontation of all, man face-to-face with himself.

[3] André Bazin, *Qu'est-ce que le Cinéma?* (Paris: Edition du Cerf, 1959), p. 90 ff.

[4] André Bazin, "The Ontology of the Photographic Image," trans. Hugh Gray, *Film Quarterly,* Summer 1960.

No longer will that confrontation be deferred on the grounds that we are too busy surviving. No longer will we be able to plead, *"Primo vivere, deinde philosophari."* The older among us will not be present when this new day dawns, but we are training those who will.

Meanwhile, we are also bringing students who came to learn first to be film makers and what that process involves, to new and interesting frontiers, to broader horizons. We are bringing them to the threshold of other studies to which the cinema is linked, or by which it is used, or in which it plays a valuable role. Among them are sociology, anthropology, epistemology, psychology, phenomenology, education, and criticism.

On the other hand, a course in aesthetics will teach students to preserve a sense of proportion in a civilization that has been called the *civilization de l'image.* While grasping the full force, the validity, the "quality" of the cinematic, they will be taught to distinguish between seeing an *image* of an orange tree, even in color, and seeing an *orange tree.*

It will remind them that while our civilization accepts, with Plato, the supremacy of the eye among the other senses because it is nearest to the "divine process" of understanding, yet our experience is not total till our sense experience is total.

In other words, we do well to examine and understand precisely what the motion-picture camera's arrival on the scene has done to our relationship to our environment, and to our environment's relationship to us.

As I presently journey along the road of this inquiry, I find myself reflecting on two statements—one by the Swiss playwright Frisch, the other by the English art critic Sir Herbert Read. Frisch has somewhere said that technology is the knack of so arranging the world that we don't have to experience it. What, I wonder, does this tell us about the cinema? "The only hope," said Sir Herbert Read, "of any amelioration in our lot lies in recognizing the biological function and supreme value of the sense of beauty."

BREAKING THE WORD BARRIER

by George C. Stoney

ABOUT TEACHING FILM in colleges I have this one great fear: that we will finally make it so acceptably academic that it will become as dull and dead as almost every other subject in the liberal arts curriculum.

I'm sure we have enough academic know-how to fractionate film study into all kinds of multiple courses in the style that has become conventional in other fields. You know the kind of thing: first it's a course in film criticism; then in the *history* of film criticism; then film criticism before 1920; then film criticism *after* 1920. (I'm citing an actual example, by the way.) Yes, we film academicians can stuff the catalogues with the best of them. But why?

Like every good English major I learned the significance of *Gammer Gurton's Needle* in the development of English drama. I read a synopsis of it in a cram book and gave the proper answer to a question about it on the comprehensive exam. But what has that kind of foolishness got to do with developing a taste for good theater? Perhaps a more direct experience with the play's text would

---

GEORGE STONEY is a writer, director, and producer of documentary films. He has taught film courses at the University of Southern California, City College of New York, Stanford University, and Columbia University. The course he describes here has been taught at Columbia University since 1958.

have meant more, but this was a survey course, and of course there wasn't time. I have a feeling that all too many of our courses are filled with film equivalents of *Gammer Gurton's Needle.*

I once had a marvelous teacher of Victorian literature, Dr. Johny Booker. He had no reputation as a scholar. He'd published almost nothing since he finished his doctoral dissertation, and when I knew him at Chapel Hill he was near retirement age. He had a terrible reputation among most of the students, because he'd always get stuck on some favorite work early in the course and never get to many of the works on which we knew we'd be given questions on the comprehensive exam.

When I took Booker's course we spent six of the ten weeks on Thomas Carlyle's *Sartor Resartus.* Dr. Booker carried us through the political and philosophic revolutions that helped shape this book. It was through this course alone that I was exposed to the work of those German philosophers whose ideas Carlyle introduced to England through his masterwork. It was Booker's close attention to Carlyle's fascination with the fresh use of words that helped me see daylight years later when I tried to find my way through Joyce's *Ulysses.* Hardly a week has gone by since then that I do not read something that is made more lucid or meaningful because I spent those ten weeks with Johny Booker.

Yet, as I say, Dr. Booker wasn't popular with students because he didn't prepare us to play the academic game. And to be honest I must acknowledge that, most of the time, students seem even keener than we teachers to play this game as conventionally as possible.

Now we do have some teachers of film with the breadth of knowledge, experience, imagination, and lonely courage that makes them capable of doing the kind of job in our field that Johny Booker did in Victorian literature. Andries Deinum is one, and those of you who may be wondering what I mean by this should read the notes and transcripts of some of Deinum's courses at the Portland Extension Center of the University of Oregon. But people like Andries Deinum can't continue unless the little academic sub-community in which they must function, honors them for this unconventional approach.

I bring all this up as a prelude to my talk, because I have a feeling a great many people in this game are so concerned about making films acceptably academic that they are quite prepared to kill and pickle them in the process.

The biggest problem I've found in film teaching is breaking through the word barrier that surrounds almost everything that's real in our lives these days, particularly on the campus. Using film as a way of transmitting meaningful sensations is quite an *un*natural as is the use of words. However, we accept this unnaturalness of words and acquire skill in their manipulation. In fact, most of our education is concerned with words in one way or another, so much so that a well educated man is described as a highly *literate* person.

Who trains us to look? We may get a smattering of this in art classes. We may get more visual training in the various fields of natural science. Yet, curiously enough, an overwhelming part of our training in the natural sciences is devoted to the acquisition of skill in translating what one sees into words. The social sciences are even more devastatingly wordbound. Soon the fresh, exciting sensations of the student's first field trip become a manipulation of polysyllabic clichés learned with great pain from all those books on the required reading list. Finally, one's doctoral dissertation is likely to be one part direct observation—reduced to words—and nine parts a recounting of a lot of other people's words.

Now, instead of jumping in and helping our colleagues out of their word-bound world, we film teachers are about to do the same thing in our own field. Fortunately we can't kill films themselves. For the mainstream of film, like the mainstream of music and literature and painting, will never flow through the groves of academe. Perhaps we should be grateful for that. But a lot of people are enrolled in our classes. Most of them come to us because they like to go to the movies. The least we owe them is a chance to sharpen their visual perception and thereby heighten their enjoyment of films. Too often all we do is increase their ability to talk about films. Words again.

I became a part-time teacher of film in 1953 after several years as a writer, director, and producer in the field, and I've continued to spend most of my time as an active film maker. I confess that I began teaching out of curiosity. I continued it as a respectable form of advertising. Now I'm thoroughly addicted to the job.

More and more these days I find myself turning to the students for help with my own films. They are quickest to remind me when I'm being pretentious or dull. Oh yes, they respond overmuch to every new style, condemning anyone who doesn't latch onto it. One soon becomes tolerant of that. But one also learns from them which films carry meaning for class after class, and which films (one's own as well as others) soon seem pointless, however stylish they might have been when they were made. Working with my students I am reminded that if I want to make films that honestly reflect the contemporary scene, I'd better go out and see afresh for myself.

So I teach because it's good for *me*. What do I give my students in return, or try to give them? Mostly, I try to help them learn a new way of seeing, a way of seeing that is peculiar to the view finder of a motion-picture camera. Nothing else is quite like it.

Please note that the course I'm about to describe, the one I have been giving at Columbia since 1958, has been developed over the years, is never two times the same, and has never been completely successful. My approach is so totally empirical, that you may get a better feeling of its nature and direction if I describe how it evolved.

When I first looked into film teaching back in the summer of 1953, I found that the classes tended to be divided into ones in which teachers took a literary approach—film history, discussion of aesthetic theory, script writing—or the purely technical approach—

camera operation, studio techniques, and mechanics of editing. Subject matter was considered of little importance. Few students had a burning desire to put anything particular on the screen. Most of them wanted to be film makers. Relatively few wanted to make films. What particularly surprised me was that most of the students didn't realize how films got produced, how subject matter is chosen, and what is involved in getting an idea from script to screen.

Most of my students that summer had been in school too long, could operate comfortably only in an academic setting, and were to frightened or lethargic to go beyond the campus unless pushed. Many of them were actually scared of people unlike themselves, which is about as poor a beginning for a film maker as I know. They wanted to read about things, write their scripts, and then mold their little set pieces in some corner of the studio or campus. When I forced them out into the street to look for themselves, and look through a view finder, most of them were disturbed. Light was supposed to be a thing that determined your "f" stop. The fact that light also changes the expression on a child's face when he is asked to look into the sun was an annoyance. Capturing the personality of that child in a series of meaningful and carefully observed and plotted incidents was a totally new concept, and they hadn't the faintest idea how one went about getting such a thing on film.

When they saw their "rushes," many of them were so disappointed they lost heart. For years they had dreamed of being film makers. Here at college they had learned to talk film, they had learned some of the mechanics of the trade, and now this! It was as if, at twenty-two years of age and as graduate students, they had written compositions at a third grade level.

What I did with that first class was to show them some of my own films and describe in the most minute detail how I went about getting these things on the screen; the human relations involved, the weather we had to deal with, the technical problems, the pressures of time and finances. How much did they learn? I don't know. Toward the end of the course one of the students said,

"Well, the one thing this course has taught me is that films don't just happen, they've got to be made." I find that the feeling behind this remark is expressed by at least half my graduate students at Columbia each year.

After a couple of summer sessions at the University of Southern California, I came for a year to the Film Institute of the City College of New York. Here I was dealing for the most part with much younger people, ones far less well mannered, but keen as mustard to get a camera into their hands and go out and shoot. I decided to let them do this before they became afraid of it, before they became such film sophisticates that they would be discouraged into impotency when they saw their first piddling efforts on the screen. The first hour in the course I showed them how to load, focus, and set the exposure on a home-movie type camera, and the second hour we went out shooting.

That same day Hans Richter, who had chosen me to succeed him at City College, had arranged (without telling me) for the two of us to confer with the Dean during this same second hour of the class. As I dashed down the steps leading my pack of eager students Richter confronted me at the bottom, demanding to know where we thought we were going. I tried to explain. He wouldn't listen. "But where is *Potemkin*?" he demanded to know. Later I learned that the first course in film at City College under Richter *always* started with a screening of *Potemkin*.

That year at City College taught me a great deal. First, I learned how thoroughly one can be deceived, and how easily students can deceive each other by the gift of gab—and New York is a talking town! By getting the students into shooting early, however, and having everyone sit in on the screening of rushes, I found I had a built-in control. Often the least verbal people had most skill in seeing with the camera and it was fascinating to see how quickly the pecking order was adjusted in consequence. (Incidentally, the ability to see with a view-finder eye seems not to correspond in any way with one's academic achievement in other fields).

Next, I learned from these students at City College the tremendous advantage of beginning active film making early. All were in their late teens, and they were much more adept with the camera in a few weeks than older students generally become in a year. They were more daring and direct in their approach to people too, and were more open to fresh approaches in editing. From this experience I am convinced that we get most of our film students too late. Delaying film production courses until they reach the graduate level is, in my opinion, a serious mistake.

It was at City College also that I learned how even the best of universities can seem more like an "ivory jungle" than an "ivory tower." Richter tried his best to teach me, but I finally trapped myself despite his best efforts. The setup was a bit peculiar, but by no means unique.

The Film Institute wanted to make its importance felt on the campus. The way to do this, following the usual academic convention, was to build up a large undergraduate enrollment so you could start a graduate program. To do *this* you gave a couple of courses in film history or appreciation that soon became known as easy electives which attracted a mass of students.

You also sought out students whom you could persuade to major in film. Those who were having trouble making the grade in other departments were always good prospects. At that time about half the students entering City College were choosing engineering. I found some of my best students had flunked out as engineers. But, by and large, I learned that this method of recruiting students was wasteful of both the students' and college's time and, I felt, simply dishonest in a good many cases.

After the first term I interviewed most of the students and discouraged those whom I thought shouldn't be taking the courses. Previous to this I had discussed the entire situation with the Dean. He agreed wholeheartedly with what I was doing. "I'm delighted to know you are interested in keeping up standards," he said. Armed with this assurance, I set to my task and succeeded in reducing our enrollment by one-third. My contract was not renewed.

Two years later I began teaching at Columbia and have been teaching there since. My course is loosely titled "Problems in the Documentary," but—like my old mentor Johny Booker—I make no attempt to cover the field. Registration is limited to twenty graduate students, which means I'm getting them too late, which means most have been in school too long, which means most of them are afraid of people. About a third are going for a master's degree in film. A few come from other departments, including journalism, medicine, anthropology, but too few for my liking. As it's a night course, running three hours one session a week for fifteen weeks, we also attract people from the fringes of the film industry and from other professional groups in the city: teachers, social workers, advertising agency employees, and public relations people working for organizations.

After the first evening I ask them all to write a film autobiography, telling me when they first became interested in film, what they've done in the field, if anything, and what they hope to get from the course. I find that practically all of them hope to be involved in film making in one way or another. However, the course I have developed with them over the past eight years is one that I am persuaded would meet the interests of a much larger body of liberal arts students who want to develop a more mature and rewarding enjoyment of films even if they never again become involved in actually making them.

I begin the course by saying, "This course costs you $150. Now if you will take that amount of money and invest it in an eight millimeter camera and film, and *think* while you're shooting, you will probably learn far more for your money than you will taking this course. The university rules say you can leave after this first session and it will cost you nothing, so I presume I won't see a good many of you after this evening. Now, if, after this evening's session, you decide to stick with the course, ley me urge you to buy, beg, or borrow, an eight millimeter camera and some raw stock (unexposed film) and shoot a film during the course. If you do you will get ten times as much from the class work, though I can't require you to do this as part of the regular assignments."

I'm glad to report that, despite my warnings, enough students keep taking the course each year to justify keeping it in the catalogue, and each year the number who do shoot their own films as the course moves along has increased. This past year all except two of them did, and it was the best class I've ever had.

Yet we spend no class time on the use of the camera or getting the right exposure or the mechanics of editing. These things the students learn on their own or from each other. Ideally I'd have an assistant of their own age to work with them on this, but figuring these things out for themselves certainly has advantages. A good many of them leave such mechanics to the blessed arbitrariness of one of those single-lens, built-in metered, battery-driven bits of wonderful junk they do so well with and that I can't abide. Actually these gadgety little cameras are almost ideal for the purposes of a course like mine, for they allow the student to concentrate most of his attention on the view finder. And it is around the view finder that I try to build my course.

In the first evening I try to impress upon them the simple fact that films are made, they don't just happen, all the propaganda of Leacock, Pennebaker, and the Maisel Brothers to the contrary notwithstanding. The second evening is usually entitled, "The View Finder Is Not Your Eye." You may think this is a self-evident truth. Most people do until they try shooting. Even then few people learn the bitter, sad, exciting, wonderful truth those six words can hold until they shoot and also view their own rushes. Once they begin to understand what these six words mean, the students are prepared to look at the world around them in a different way, and we start to work in earnest.

Each student is required to select some subject about which he wants to make a film, to research it, to develop it as a film treatment, and to talk it over with me. Once we do this, he outlines the production, which means he finds and tests out all the locations, casts it, budgets it, and schedules the shooting. Finally, he either shoots the film or writes it as a finished script with the main sequences sketched out in frames drawn from the chosen locations. All this work is done outside class hours, usually on weekends. Except for the final two sessions, seldom more than an hour of class time is devoted to a review of the work. While most of the students work alone or with people who aren't in the class, this direct experience with the medium soon begins to dominate the whole course.

Once they are launched on their projects we begin to examine in some detail how other film makers have done their job. In session three, for example, which I call "Reality and the Film Poet," we contrast Colin Lowe's magnificent *Corral* with a long documentary called *Back of Beyond.* I find this last film particularly good for beginning students because its virtues and lapses in taste are so obvious. I find I can often make a point better with an imperfect film than with a perfect one; one more reason why I don't hesitate to show the class my own films along with others. Session four has, since 1958, been devoted to the idea of "Cinéma Vérité," though we weren't using that term way back before *Toby and the Tall Corn* was made, and I was screening such pioneer efforts as Fonzionelli and Leo Herwitz' *Story of a Fighter.* Of late I've found it useful to give the class a direct contrast such as Lindsey Anderson's *Every Day Except Christmas* to emphasize the virtues and limitations of this approach.

By session five the students have been struggling with their own script problems sufficiently for me to use their experience in class. So we begin with Zavattini's idea of "the found story" and move on to our own immediate problems of scripting reality for its essence and not its tedium. By session six many of the students are facing the prospect of having to go out and film their scripted ideas. Because most of them have chosen to do films about "real people" (with considerable prodding from me, I admit) we have a session that begins with the question, "Is man's face private property?" We examine here the whole matter of the film maker's obligation to the people whom he puts on the screen—a subject I find peculiarly unpopular among a distressing number of my own professional colleagues.

In session seven we examine some film makers' techniques for presenting didactic films under the title, "The Story With a Moral." Session eight is devoted to the use of comedy for didactic purposes. Sessions nine and ten examine several political and propaganda films, trying to highlight their differing techniques by screening them in context. In session eleven we study three films, which concern a time of decision for their leading characters, in order to contrast the directors' personal approaches to emotional experiences. Session twelve again emphasizes different film treatments of a similar subject—New York City. Session thirteen, entitled "The Heart and the Head," analyzes a series of films which, if made by less thoughtful people, could have been merely sensational or repellent. In each case the material is handled to produce not a surface, immediate, overt response, but something stronger and deeper. The final two sessions are usually reserved for review, aided, when possible, by group examination of certain of the class projects.

I always make my current productions as much a part of the course as I do theirs. They read my scripts, hear my reports of triumphs and tragedies from the previous week's struggle with production. I often show them my rough cuts and demonstrate with my own failures. This last spring, for example, I had to return on two occasions to a distant mountain location to get additional footage because of some fairly elementary mistakes in planning plus the usual bit of hard luck. They saw the reasons for this on the screen, saw me correct the errors, and learned what the effort cost in money, time, and worry.

The students learn even more from each other, everything from actual camera operation to the way to wangle free transportation from the New York City Parks Department. It's gratifying to see how quickly they are persuaded by another student's example to try for themselves. No teacher's example, it seems, is quite so persuasive.

I've never been able to predict who in the group will come up with the most interesting work. Academic background, urbanity, professional competence in other fields, all seem to be quite unreliable as guides. One forty-ish yet naive maiden school teacher announced to the class a couple of years ago that she wanted to make a film about a tree. Undisturbed by the titters from the back of the room she went on to explain that she wanted to make a film about a *very special* tree, the big Norway spruce they had chosen to decorate for Christmas in Rockefeller Center. She came to the next session of the class with an ancient camera which some shrewd dealer had sold to her. By this time we were all feeling a bit sorry for her, but she wasn't discouraged. The next session she reported on a trip she had made to see the tree as it stood in the forest near Hurley, New York. It seems she had talked her way into the Public Relations Department at Rockefeller Center, wangled a ride up to the woods, and had been invited to spend the weekend with the farm family who were supplying the tree.

By the time the tree was ready to be felled and trucked on a block-long trailer into the city, this shy, inexperienced film maker had a place reserved for herself in the cab that pulled it. She, alone, was allowed to film inside the workmen's barrier when the tree was hoisted into place in New York City. I saw her there with her little camera when I watched the event on TV.

The lady's film, though technically very crude, did catch the excitement of the event and reflected some of the very human experiences she had enjoyed in making it.

I try to discourage them from making the standard kind of joke films, the parodies, the introspective existential love bits and such which are the favorite doodlings of college cineasts. Rather, I try to persuade them to choose a subject that is important to them or which they will find interesting and enlightening for itself. This last year students chose such varied subjects as: fashion therapy for girls in a mental hospital; preserving the landmarks of New York from the bulldozer; the smoke-abatement campaign; my Cape Cod home in the wintertime; teaching kindergarten in a slum neighborhood; a lonely hearts club; a protest march to Washington; an oceanographic investigation on Long Island; the story of a racing car.

The poorest film was made by a mature student who had the most impressive academic record. He spoke well, did excellent written work, and was generally recognized throughout the early sessions as the group's natural leader. He organized his production well and showed initiative in researching it. So we were all shocked when we viewed his "rushes." He kept trying but it was soon obvious that he had no notion of how one caught an idea in a view finder and probably never would. Yet this man enjoyed seeing films. He could make quite intelligent comments about them.

My implied assumption that people's tastes in film will be improved when they have direct experience with production is certainly one that can be questioned on a number of grounds. Perhaps Aaron Copland got to the heart of this argument when he made the following comment in his delightful book *What to Listen for in Music:*

> Certain schools of thought are inclined to stress the value for the listener of some practical experience of music. They say, in effect, play *Old Black Joe* on the piano with one finger and it will get you closer to the mysteries of music than reading a dozen volumes. No harm can be done, certainly, from playing the piano a bit or even from playing it moderately well. But as an introduction to music I am suspicious of it, if only because of the many pianists who spend their lives playing great works, yet whose understanding of music is, on the whole, rather weak.[1]

My reply is that Copland and I may be talking about two kinds of enjoyment. I have no more interest in filling the country with

[1] Rev. ed.; New York: New American Library of World Literature, 1963. P. 17.

fifth-rate film makers than he has in filling it with fifth-rate pianists. But we do face the fact, in the film world at least, that more and more of our information is coming to us via film and TV; more and more of our education, our entertainment, our propaganda, our advertising; more and more of our "communication" to use that deadly collective.

Somehow we learn about words. Few do about film. Moreover, the use of film and TV is now so widespread that a surprisingly large number of people in other professions already find themselves in positions where they need to know how to work with film makers. Doctors, social workers, journalists, psychologists, they are all trying to use film now, and most are making a bad job of it because they don't know how to begin to think in film terms. And the film makers with whom they work haven't time to absorb their clients' special knowledge and points of view.

Eventually I'd like to see our courses attracting more people from other departments of the university so these specialists can make their own films as they now write their own books, helped along, to be sure, by professional editors. In the past we have tended to make our specialty into a kind of sacred cult. You were a film maker and that's all, or you were an unwelcome dabbler, whatever your skill in other fields. This is all foolishness, of course.

Here are some limitations in my course I'm still struggling with.

First, students are required to supply their own equipment, although eight millimeter cameras now cost less than the microscopes and typewriters most high schools furnish their students routinely. At present Columbia's production courses are set up around 16-mm. equipment, and there has been no indication that this will change. One could hardly afford to allow students the kind of full-time use of equipment I have described if it costs as much as 16-mm. items do.

Second, while the films are made entirely outside class time, the instructor must budget a lot of his own time beyond the class period to review the films and "rushes" with the students. Much of the learning happens during these sessions, and they are not the kind of thing one can pass on to an assistant, if, indeed, one were made available.

Third, while my class tends to attract a group of unusually conscientious students, the end of the term finds a large number of people with unfinished films. Nobody has any idea how long it takes to make a film until he trys it. I explain this at the beginning of the course but no one believes me.

That's the course. Certainly what I have described is no substitute for those big, easy-elective courses many departments continue to offer to build up enrollment without straining the faculty budget needed for graduate production courses. Frankly, I'm glad I don't have to wrestle with the kind of academic bookkeeping that seems to make these classes necessary. Because I don't, my somewhat caustic remarks may seem both naive and irresponsible to those of you who do have such responsibilities. Yet, I would like to observe that when we set ourselves up on tax-exempt, publicly supported campuses, when we collect the fees we do from parents and—most important—when we occupy big hunks of the students' time during the most important years of their lives, we have no right to kid them into thinking they are getting an education when they aren't. The fact that a lot of other university departments are doing the same thing is the poorest kind of excuse.

Above all, let's stop killing people's enthusiasm for film with survey courses in film history given in badly blacked-out halls with poor speakers where even the greatest film ever made hasn't a chance. As a film maker I resent this more than anything else, and I know from personal experience that our colleges—yes our film schools themselves—are setting an abysmal standard in projection.

There's no law that says we *have* to teach film in colleges. Quite often our students would be better off if we didn't.

Supplementary List

Editor's note: The following films and suggested reading assignments were associated with the course Professor Stoney has described when it was taught at Columbia University in 1963:

SESSION I

Films for analysis:

Mint Tea, 20 min. Produced and directed by Pierre Kafan. French.

Children Who Draw Pictures, 44 min. Directed by Fufumi Hani. Japanese.

The Fur Lined Foxhole, (first 12 min.). Produced and directed by the instructor.

Suggested reading:

Cocteau, Jean, *The Autobiography of a Film.*

SESSION II

Films for analysis:

All My Babies, 58 min. Written and directed by the instructor.

Muscle Beach, 10 min. Written and directed by Irving Lerner and Joseph Stritch. American.

Suggested reading:

Jennings, Humphrey, "Notes for a Film on the London Symphony," in *Film Quarterly,* Winter 1961–62.

SESSION III

Films for analysis:

Corral, 12 min. Colin Lowe and Wolfe Koenig. Canadian.

Back of Beyond, (parts, total running time is 65 min.). Directed by John Heyer. Australian.

The Backbreaking Leaf, 27 min. Written and directed by Terence D. McCartney-Filgate. Canadian.

Suggested reading:

Griffith, Richard, *The World of Robert Flaherty.*

Eastman Kodak, *Guide to Better Movie Making.*

SESSION IV

Films for analysis:

Lonely Boy, 27 min. Wolfe Koenig and Roman Kroiter. Canadian.
Primary, 30 min. Richard Leacock and associates. American.
Every Day Except Christmas, 40 min. Lindsey Anderson. British.

Suggested reading:

Reisz, Karel, *Technique of Film Editing.*
Marcorelle, Louis, "Nothing but the Truth," in *Sight and Sound,* Summer 1963.
Interview with Peter Brooke in same issue.

SESSION V

Films for analysis:

Kail Nihta Socrates ("Good Night, Socrates"), 34 min. Maria Moraites and Stuart Hagmann. American.
Bunker Hill, '56, 26 min. Kent Mackenzie and associates. American.

Suggested Reading:

Kracauer, Siegfried, "The Found Story," in *Film Culture,* Winter 1958.
Kracauer, Siegfried, "The Spectator," and Zavattini, Cesare, "How I Did Not Make Italia Mia," in *Film: Book 1,* ed. by Robert Hughes.

SESSION VI

Films for analysis:

The Newcomers, 28 min. By the instructor.
Prisoner at Large, (51 min., probably half of this). Bill Jersey. American.

Suggested reading:

Griffin, John Howard, *Black Like Me,* a journalistic report currently being made into a feature by two experienced documentary film makers. At the next—or some future—session there will be a discussion of the handling of the ethical problems involved in personal privacy by this journalist and the much more difficult one faced by the men who are turning the book into a film.

SESSION VII

Films for analysis:

The Grievance, 28 min. Directed by Morton Parker. Canadian.

Psychiatric Nursing, 35 min. Written by Ruth and Ralph Schoolman. Directed by Lee Bobker. American.

The Language of Faces, 20 min. John Korty.

Suggested reading:

Goodman, Paul, "Designing Pacifist Films," in *Film: Book 2, Films of Peace and War,* ed. by Robert Hughes. (Other material in this volume may also be of interest.)

SESSION VIII

Films for analysis:

Falls, 5 min. One in a series called "Accidents Don't Happen." Directed by John Mulhallen. Canadian.

Massingham Films, (6 one-minute shorts designed for theaters in England during World War II) plus *Pool of Contentment.* Written and directed by Richard Massingham, M.D. English.

Walk With Me, 18 min. By the instructor.

Suggested reading:

Eastman, Max, *The Anatomy of Laughter.*

SESSION IX

Films for analysis:

Operation Abolition, (original 45 min. version). Produced by George Johnson. Written and edited under the supervision of Fulton Lewis III. American.

Sunday, 16 min. Dan Draison. American.

The Walk, (part of 40 min.). Hillary Harris and others.

Suggested reading:

"The Issue," in *Film: Book 2, Films of Peace and War,* ed. by Robert Hughes.

SESSION X

Films for analysis:

Harvest of Shame, (parts of 54 min.). Edward R. Murrow and David Lowe.

Clinton and the Law, (parts of 60 min.). Edward R. Murrow and Fred Friendly.

Sit In, (parts of 54 min.). With Chet Huntley.

Suggested reading:

Scripts for *Let There Be Light* and *Night and Fog* as printed in *Film: Book 2, Films of Peace and War,* ed. by Robert Hughes, recommended chiefly to demonstrate how little of the emotional impact of these films is conveyed in the printed form.

SESSION XI

Films for analysis:

Moment to Act, 28 min. Directed by Roger Tilton. American.

Blood and Fire, 30 min. Directed by Terence D. McCartney-Filgate. Canadian.

The Mischief Makers, 27 min. Directed by Francois Truffaut. French.

Suggested reading:

Reread a novel you would most like to see turned into a motion picture, bearing in mind the problems of film style discussed in the past ten sessions.

White, E. B., "New York," an essay that first appeared in *Holiday Magazine* and was subsequently published as a small volume. Next week we will see a film based on this essay.

SESSION XII

Films for analysis:

E. B. White's New York, 54 min. Directed by Robert K. Sharpe for "The Seven Lively Arts" program.

N.Y., N.Y., 15 min. By Francis Thompson.

How to Look at a City, 28 min. Work print of instructor's work-in-progress for National Educational Television series "Metropolis: Creator or Destroyer?"

Suggested reading:

Mannes, Marya, *The New York I Love.*

Miller, Warren, *The Cool World.*

SESSION XIII

Films for analysis:

Overture, 9 min. Produced by Thorold Dickinson. The U.N.

The Steps of Age, 35 min. By Ben Maddow and Sidney Meyers. American.

Paul Tompkowitz, 10 min. By Colin Lowe, Wolfe Koenig and Roman Kroiter.

Day After Day, 30 min. The National Film Board French unit. Canadian.

Glass, 10 min. By Carl Hanstra. Dutch.

Suggested reading:

Schary, Dore (with Charles Palmer), *The Story of a Film,* "The Next Voice You Hear."

SESSIONS XIV and XV

Review of class film projects.

COMMENTS

DOUBTS

by John E. Burchard

LET ME START by trying to establish what I shall *not* be discussing. With a single exception I am *not* talking about the education of technicians in the making of film.

The exception I would make is along the lines of Mr. Stoney's film making but not for the reasons he enumerates. I am not convinced that a little dabbling in the technique of an art makes anyone a more sensitive observer of the masterpieces of that art. General Eisenhower's taste in the arts has, for example, probably not been elevated one whit by his Sunday painting. On this question I side with Aaron Copland. And although I have often said that we need to do more about the visual training of those we educate, I do not see why training people to look at things through a view finder is in any way fundamental. Rather, the reason for early film-making experience is that too much of our education postpones too long any opportunity for the young student to engage himself immediately in what he believes to be his primary interests. If the student *really* is enamored of film he ought to be able to shoot some very early in his education, and he should not be stopped if

---

JOHN E. BURCHARD is Dean Emeritus of Humanities and Social Sciences at Massachusetts Institute of Technology and Visiting Professor (head of the Department of Design) at the University of California, Berkeley. He is an architectural historian, a Fellow and former president of the American Academy of Arts and Sciences, and has been a member of the Advisory Board of the Aspen Institute for ten years.

he is doing well because of some silly notion that this is not an educational experience.

I suspect that the low quality of most commercial films is not because they are deliberately made to match a presumed low taste of audiences, but because most of those who write, act, produce, direct, and distribute are themselves, whatever their airs, men and women of scant and impoverished life experience, of limited education, of ingrained and then carefully nourished parochial bad taste, and, in consequence, of an extremely confused notion as to what is profound or important. Thus in some respects they come off worst when they try the hardest.

I could not help thinking as Mr. Fischer enumerated his examples of cinematic metaphors, how obvious, even banal they were; the panther, the headless Venus, the steam whistle, the beehive. Are they obvious because the film makers deliberately chose allusions they hoped the viewers would understand (something every great writer has respected) or because the film makers themselves could think of nothing more subtle? I suspect the latter. A good general education might alleviate some of this although it will not, of course, provide talent where talent does not exist.

I am talking about a place in a particular sun for courses on film. The particular sunny place, hopefully a respected place, is in the liberal arts elective curriculum. You are asking for a great deal when you ask for this, and your responsibility is not lessened because much junk has already accumulated there, at least in some institutions. Why are you asking for a great deal? In a typical undergraduate experience, something between thirty-two and forty half-year subjects will be encountered. Of these something between twenty-four and thirty will be pre-empted by preliminary distributional and subsequent major requirements. This leaves you to compete for one-eighth to one-tenth of the student's free time if you propose a half-year course and for one-fourth to one-fifth if you talk about a year's course. This is a serious responsibility and no member of the teaching community is relieved of it simply because somebody else has been careless. That many of our curricula contain trivial electives justifies nobody in increasing this stockpile.

I am not a film buff. I do not voraciously consume all the films that come along. They have to queue up for my attention along with many other achievements in the arts and of the intellect. When I go to *avant garde* films and approve them, it is exactly as I go to *avant garde* paintings. I go to satisfy my curiosity; I approve if they seem to me to offer something of significant *content* or *comment* and not because they are displays of technique or personality or merely because they are new and occasionally different or perchance fashionable.

As a second disqualifier you ought to know that I do not consider Sam Goldwyn, Louis Mayer, or Cecil B. deMille or Joseph E. Levine to have been titans save in their own little narcissistic frog ponds. They have about the same half-life, in my view, as Daniel Frohman or Lee Shubert or David Belasco and a considerably shorter one than Lord Beaverbrook or William Randolph Hearst. They deserve about as much of a student's attention as would be accorded them in a general history of the communications industry or in a survey history by the Beards—no more, and this obviously would not be very much.

I am even less interested in the Frank Sinatras or the Elizabeth Taylors and their vulgar conduct; or in efforts to blow up the problems of Marilyn Monroe or Jean Harlow into those of an Antigone or an Electra. (I read an explanation of Carol Baker's failure in *Harlow* that said she had no sense of tragedy!) Study of the caprices and the mishaps of these great nonactors is irrelevant, save as the shortest kind of footnote to a course in American sociology where the interest would be not in that they behaved as they did, but in why so many people seemed to care.

Despite all these strictures, I have managed by some mysterious process to identify and see practically all the films that are generally listed at conferences like this one. Moreover I have been doing this for a long time, almost since babyhood when I viewed the serial about Africa which was replete with Kathleen Williams and lions, or the more "advanced" one about the *Perils of Pauline,* through the early comics of Sennett and Chaplin, to the days when we went to a little house near the Chicago stockyards to see *The Cabinet of Dr. Caligari.* I have kept on doing this right down to date, and most of the time for the past half-century. I have seen films at the moment when they were current, although naturally I have filled in a few lacunae in the basement of the Museum of Modern Art. I think I have had a fairly thorough exposure to what might generally be agreed to be the great literature of the film and over reflective time.

Professor Ellis provided me with a text when he began talking about a "beginning course at an advanced level" which would try to combine the technological and the business and, perhaps by inference, the sociological and the psychological settings with the aesthetics and then went on to say, "In a course in literary criticism one doesn't go into the state of the publishing industry or the technology of printing, the merchandising methods of booksellers, or the interests and organizational affiliations of readers—though a case might be made for doing so." I wish he had made the case. It might have spared me the necessity of exploring whether one can, in fact, be made.

From the point of view of one group of "purist" teachers in the fine arts, it is only the end product that matters. You look at what Leonardo's unfinished *Pietà* says to you today. You may be able to look more perceptively if your eyes can remain unclouded by knowledge or conjecture as to the state of Catholic belief about the Crucifixion at his moment of time, or his own belief, or the nature of his patrons, or where he got his stone, or what the capacities of his tools were, or why he didn't finish. Then if the art is uninteresting in today's terms it can be ignored, at least for now. There is a great deal to be said for this view. Some of us think that it is too narrow a view and that the experience is richer if something more can be added. But it may well be that when we add it, what we add is social or political history or something else and only remotely related to art, just as the additions to physics made by Galileo can be counted without reference to his political ineptitude in the fact of Cardinal Boramini, or Newton's without apologizing for his theological absurdities. All these examples tell us is that a great thinker in some area may be a fool in another, which may not be a trivial lesson. But this is not what we were seeking when first we encountered the *Pietà*. So it is, no doubt, in secondary or at least in other rubrics that all this sort of material belongs, and not in the rubric of aesthetics. I have a solid suspicion that a good deal of what is tucked into alleged courses on the aesthetics of the cinema is of this sort, and I cannot help asking why.

There is too much disposition in the apologists of film courses to suggest that film is so different from other arts that direct confrontation is not enough. Even Mr. Fischer's early lectures seem to me to suffer from this belief. Surely if we had to spend much time understanding how an Elizabethan playwright had to produce his play before we engaged *Hamlet,* many of us might never have engaged him. But *Hamlet* is our main interest, not the sociology and economics and politics of the Elizabethan theater. The limitations imposed on an artist are not a defense against bad art or a laurel for good.

I should confess right now that in my own courses in architectural history I feel that I have to supply the surroundings, lest the architectural monument which is of the central interest be abstracted out of life. But this is because, though all arts are in a sense social arts, architecture is the supreme social art and buildings are quite unlikely to be commissioned for nonpurposes. Architecture is part utilitarian and has to be measured in part by utility, a measure which should not, I think, be applied to the other arts including the art of film. But even here I must be careful not to become bemused by the fascinating details, not to let the machinations of Abbot Suger rise higher than the vaults of St. Denis.

I should be disposed to let a course on film into the free elective meadows, only if I felt that its proponents had sufficient confidence in the contents of the films themselves. I would want them to be sure that the films were so rich in comment on significant human experience that no necessity was felt to add other things in order to justify the course; that films of grandeur would justify themselves just as works of grandeur in other fields justify themselves, towering so high for the perceptive student that the stupid teacher could not in fact destroy them.

This ability of enough films to stand firmly on the pedestal of contents would be the only thing that would dispose me to admit a course about them. There are important things to be learned about the sociology of films and film audiences and even film makers. But whether you like it or not these belong in courses of sociology, and how much space they take is better left to sociologists than to film enthusiasts. There are no doubt important aspects of film as communication that belong in courses on mass media or broader ones on communication, but the decision as to how much belongs and where in such a matrix should be left in other hands. There are aspects of the film industry which may belong in business and managerial history. Again, others should decide. By "others" I mean sociologists, psychologists, professors of business administration who should be in charge of courses in sociology, psychology, business. And the lives of the makers of film probably belong nowhere in serious college curricula unless as examples of abnormal or adolescent behavior in some courses of psychology and perhaps psychiatry. In my judgment you should not try to put all these things into your own ball of wax though you may have some responsibility to see that the others do not ignore them. Mr. Fischer is to commended for leaving such things out of his course.

A number of the syllabi presented here seem to me to have been doomed to superficiality whether taught by a single reasonably well-informed generalist or by specialists coming in new and fresh week by week. Even Mr. Fischer's course seems to me guilty on this count. I should not think much of a literature course that tried to deal with the novel, the short story, the poem, the play, and the essay all in one package and from many different countries and styles at that; or the course in the visual arts that tried to say anything serious about etchings, lithographs, photographs, paintings, bas reliefs, mosaics, and sculpture plus architecture, all in one package. Why then all this in a single film course? Is it perhaps because there are not enough first class examples of one genre alone to engage the serious attention of a class, even for a semester?

Mr. Knight's course seems to me much better by the standards I am setting because a good deal of miscellaneous lore has been excluded. It therefore seems more cohesive and defensible. But it bothers me because it finally runs into the same difficulties though perhaps in a more sophisticated way. I do not accept his statement that the short span of cinema development and its proximity to our own times constitutes a total advantage to the marriage of means and ends in an art course. To connect them up is not that hard in the other arts, and one can also overdo an interest in technology.

However naive the people of the date of *The Great Train Robbery* may have been, what they had to say extended far beyond the technological capacities of the film makers to say. Thus *The Great Train Robbery* does not communicate either about the eternal human as *Hamlet* does or a lot about humans of its own time as *Great Expectations* does. The most it can show us is the state of an art at a moment. This impairs the total importance of Mr. Knight's early examples. At the other end, in the *avant garde,* technique again transcends, but for quite opposite reasons; the technique now seems to outrun the power of the director to use it.

But at the middle the technique does match the ideas and this is a very fat middle. In this fat middle the films are long, and if one is dealing seriously with an idea course, one cannot stomach looking at samples from several, but must rather experience the whole work on the general principle that works which are not worthwhile considering as a whole are unlikely to be worthwhile considering in excerpts, and that it is better to miss many great works altogether than to encounter them all abridged by people who could not have written or directed a line of them. So the teacher or the student will have to make choices in the list Mr. Knight provides each week. Surely it matters which choice is made. If some of the class have chosen *Wild Strawberries*, *The World of Apu*, some *Rashomon* and some *8½*, what discussion is possible save at the level of technique? And if a single one is chosen for all, which one? In this case the discussion can concentrate on meaning and not method.

But in the end we must ask, if we were to choose one film a week from Mr. Knight's list, whether each would, in fact, yield a content experience equivalent in depth and subtlety to that provided in a course in another art spread over the same sixty or seventy years, say literature or painting or even architecture. I venture to suggest that it really would not be competitive in depth even in our own times, let alone the times of Sophocles or Dante or the Tudors or the Enlightenment.

It is perhaps worth a moment to think of our own times which are the times of film. It is now just a little more than fifty years since Parisiana, The King of the Cinemas was built in Paris. Yesterday on the plane from San Francisco, I jotted down the names of some of the people who have walked the stages of painting, writing, and composing since 1913. The lists are from the top of my head and surely partial. But listen to them and weep.

Painters from 1913:

Picabia, Léger, Mondrian, Klee, Kandinsky, Arp, Breton, Rouault, most of Picasso, much of Braque, Schlemmer, Grosz, Schwitters, Orozco, Rivera, Tamayo, Marin, Prendergast, Stuart Davis, de Kooning, Rothko, Tobey, Motherwell, Kline.

Writers from 1913:

Proust, Valéry, Mauriac, Gide, Claudel, Colette, Apollinaire, Cocteau, Joyce, D. H. Lawrence, Huxley, Mann, Hesse, Fitzgerald, Hemingway, Faulkner, Wolfe, MacLeish, T. S. Eliot, Pound, Sartre, Camus, Malraux, Moravia.

Composers:

Stravinsky, Prokofiev, Schönberg, Bartok, Berg, Webern, Milhaud, Hindemith, Honegger, Sessions, Copland, Piston, Foss, and most all of the great jazzmen.

Can we honestly claim as much for film? And if we cannot, may this not account for the grab-bag nature of many proposed film courses because consciously or intuitively their designers know that there is not enough in film content to justify something different. I hope this is not so. I am sure most of you will insist it is not.

Suppose we were to compare a study of the Cathedral of Amiens or Joyce's *Ulysses* with one of *Citizen Kane* or *The Armored Cruiser, Prince Potemkin,* or *8½*. In the cathedral or the book there are multitudes of things, big and small, explicit and implicit, trivial and important, specialized and generalized. The richness of the storeshouse is almost inexhaustible. It cannot only provide many stimuli for *all* of us, but also an enormous variety of special stimuli for *each* of us, private worlds, if you like, subject to investigation at a variety of levels. This is of course what characterizes great works of the visual arts, of literature, of theater. Is there really such an array of riches in *Kane* or *Potemkin;* is Fellini really such an observer as Joyce? Without the potentials of *Ulysses, mutatis mutandis,* a proposed subject may be barren and can properly be challenged as a part of liberal education.

So, abandoning technique to technicians and anecdotal or apocryphal history to antiquarians and the columnists, we come squarely to the question of content and excellence. We must demand of film, if it is to be taken seriously as a contender for student attention (I am not talking of how many may register for it because that, alas, is no measure of its merit); we must ask that it pit itself against drama from Aeschylus to Brecht, against literature from Homer to Sartre, art from Lascaux to Picasso and so on. This is not a matter of the span of time, but of the number of really significant landmarks which can be found, enough, say, to provide the fodder for a single semester's course. Youth cannot be a defense for scarcity. A usefully chastening exercise for the proponents of film courses in general courses would be to see if they could list enough films from *the whole film library* which, shorn of technique and history, would be important enough to stand comparison even for a semester with the main works of Aeschylus, Sophocles, Euripides, Aristophanes, Homer, Virgil, Dante, Shakespeare, Molière, Goethe, and so on.

If we assert such stands, manifestly we will select only a few films, but that does not mean that we can select none. The thing is not to be carried away by our enthusiasm into promoting, even over-selling the trivial; into believing for example that Orson Welles is a profound thinker, that the symbolism of *Citizen Kane*'s sled is in the same league as the iconography of Amiens, the images in Dante's *Commedia* or even the lesser number in *Moby Dick* or *Ulysses;* that the portrayal of a man in *Citizen Kane* is even to be compared with that say in *Le Rouge et le Noir* or *The Great Gatsby.* If such parallels cannot fairly be drawn is it not fair to ask whether a student be enticed into the consideration of *Citizen Kane* who has not encountered the *Commedia,* into *Fantasia* who does not know Tintorretto and the *9th Symphony,* into *The Tramp* who has had no experience with *Don Quixote de la Mancha* or *Gulliver's Travels?* Where are the film encounters which can, in effect and in their own way provide comparable levels of experience? I do not make the judgment that they do not exist. Nor do I suggest you leave the decision to the pundits of other disciplines who may without experience and acting as uninformed snobs who know without looking that films are not good, rule against you. All I ask is that you police your own enthusiasms by comparative criticism.

I know from personal experience how many professors of the older humanities, and educators and administrators, think they know all about films without ever having experienced them, and are proud of their narrow, uninformed prejudices against film. I know of the stupidity of a great university which has gravely decreed that its students may indulge in film making for one year for limited credit but no more, so that the talented youngster has little alternative but to leave. Mr. Stoney is right to see no reasons why cameras should not be as available free as electron microscopes. It is a shame that Mr. Knight has to warn that film rentals might cost $300. More money than that is spent on broken chemistry beakers regularly.

These are hard barriers to break but they should be broken. Could not some of these doubts and enthusiasms be put to the test? If the old fogies of literature, history, and philosophy are against films through ignorance, they ought to be educated. Suppose through the benefice of a private foundation twenty first-class representatives of the established arts in liberal curricula were assembled with three or four of you in a pleasant place like Aspen, Hanover, Mexico City, or even Santa Barbara. Suppose you had picked fifteen or so film classics on which you were willing to rest your case for eminent content. Suppose each was screened and followed by an extended colloquium on the value of the content as compared with the value of contents in the other fields. If they reported favorably, you would have won an important skirmish; if they remained unconvinced, perhaps you ought to think again.

I am pretty sure that you will be able to wedge even more courses about film into the curriculum than now are there, but I don't congratulate you for the academic political skill or persistence or whatever will bring it about. You should not expect to make progress by pejorative exaggerations like the one with which Mr. Stoney began that almost every subject in the liberal arts curriculum is dull and dead. This is simply not so. In the end you have got to be interested not in the admission to the curriculum but in the mounting of courses which are properly valued in the highest hierarchies of the elective curriculum.

It is an important step forward as Mr. Gray has realized that the time spent on viewing should not be classroom time but comparable in all respects to the preparatory time a student must spend for example in the perusal of literary texts, or the solving of assigned problems on mathematics. But even with this strengthening improvement, the superior rating will never be gained so long as your courses are conceived as courses about the world of film, but only when film has really important things to say about the world, and especially about the human world. And only, moreover, when these films can be called masterpieces, good enough in form and content to compare with the best other works of man and to contain so much that it is profitable to examine them at length, and at leisure, and at many levels.

This is certainly not so with film used as historical reflection

A CRITIQUE
AND SOME COMMENTS ON CREATING AN AMERICAN FILM INSTITUTE

by Colin Young

THERE WILL BE two strains running through my argument. *I* find these strains at conflict myself, and much of my teaching is an attempt to resolve this conflict. On the one hand, George Stoney is surely right when he complains about academic deadness. I did not detect that he was complaining about academicism, or the academy, but professional deadness. We all complain about Hollywood's pose, the trade's pose in general, but this does not mean we wish to abandon the profession. But we have some evidence of academic deadness, and I mean this in the kindest way, since we are stuck, in the American university system, with the system of tenure, and the privileges that go with it. We know the pressures put upon young professors to publish, or perish. But the *Journal* of the Society of Cinematologists might be a place in which to publish *and* perish.

On the other hand, and this is the second strain, there is an irrational quality to art which irritates and confounds those who are trying to put knowledge of art into systems. That is why art studies

---

COLIN YOUNG is Associate Professor of Theatre Arts and Chairman of the Theatre Arts Department at the University of California, Los Angeles. He holds master's degrees from St. Andrews University and U.C.L.A. He has been a cameraman, editor, and writer in Hollywood, and writes frequently about films and film making.

sometimes seem out of place in the academy, and why so much pressure is put upon teachers of film by colleagues in other departments, to adopt their methodology. In many other disciplines, especially in the humanities, scholars seek causal lines to explain everything, for without the patterns which emerge with this approach they fear they have no subject, there is no intellectual content, and they do not belong in an academy. Unable to resolve this dilemma, many excellent teachers leave the academy, and others capitulate, before they have really identified the nature of the problem facing them.

Film professors, put in this position, often try to make themselves respectable by conforming to what they think is expected of them. This uneasiness shows in the papers offered here by many of the professional teachers. But I do not think we should rely solely on these papers, any more than their authors do in class. To a great extent these course outlines *must* appear ridiculous, cut off from the films which provide the context. In the presence of the films we all improvise, and our best stuff is not written down. It takes a very special kind of teacher to remember after the event what created the excitement, and if he tries to write it down, he will more often than not sound more stilted on paper than he does in class.

I suggest that we cannot conduct our courses in film history as if we were in the humanities—at least not in the humanities departments that I am most familiar with. It is not only that we can argue that Shakespeare did not *know* all about iambic pentameters—he simply wrote them, and why should students approach him from that point of view, rather than from a consideration of his plays as something to be performed. It is also that we are dealing always with primary material in a history course—because we are showing this primary source to the students. We *have* to think of them as audience as well as class. We cannot assume in advance that we know more about a film's merit than they do. Art is democratic as well as mysterious, and we can easily become very bad teachers by being dogmatic before we have earned the right to be so. We are often closer to the sciences in a laboratory session than we are to the humanities in a quiz section. It is not always good film pedagogy to begin with concepts and then turn to film; it may very often have to be the other way about.

If we cram too much into our courses, as John Burchard complains we do, this may mean we don't know what we are doing, and are filling in the holes of a limited subject; but it also may mean that there is a great deal of material to cover, and that we are simply not expert enough yet in knowing how to organize it. When I read Jack Ellis' paper, I was sorry he felt he had to apologize for including production as well as aesthetics. I would make the contrary objection to Ellis' course—and that is that it has too much aesthetics in it for a survey course. Once again we are presented with the problem of too much—not too little as Mr. Burchard complains. Mr. Burchard also begs the whole question against film study when he argues that anything of value in many of these courses really borrows that value from the other discipline it conjoins with. Why should we be surprised when subjects overlap? It is to the discredit of neither. Catalogue writers don't have the last word on how knowledge is compartmentalized. I spend a lot of my time with sociologists, because I find we are grappling with the same questions. Earlier, I would have thought to find more interest in what I was doing among the painters and humanists—but I don't mind that they have other interests so long as they leave me alone to mine.

Mr. Burchard says: "This ability of enough films to stand firmly on the pedestal of contents would be the only thing that would dispose me to admit a course about them." He doesn't mean by content what film makers mean, I fancy. If we are concerned with content, and pedestal-level content at that, then we can presumably proceed on the assumption that all the proper academic methods for dealing with this content will apply, and that there is not much difference between film scholarship and any other kind of scholarship.

There is much work to be done in building up reliable factual knowledge about inventions, origins, priorities, credits, synopses, and so on. The good work of this kind, however, is being done outside the universities—by George Pratt, Gordon Hendricks, and Kemp Niver, for example. But before we can do it according to our own relevant patterns, Mr. Burchard again discourages us, by disparaging technological developments and the archetypes of Porter and others, as irrelevant to any decent interest. But it is simply *not* relevant to ask a film teacher to justify his time by asking himself if it is right to take the students away from *King Lear.* We begin with the hypothesis that film is important and go on doing so until proven wrong. It is not enough to wave landmarks in English drama at us.

There is another area of film research which has very little to do with traditional methods, because it does not deal with the film as a static object, but with it as it exists for an audience. "You can't look at the same film twice," could be a good Heraclitean motto for teachers of film appreciation courses. The consideration of films as events, rather than as facts, leads us into a more lively form of history, and into aesthetics. It might be good if we made a general rule to identify in our writings and lectures, those films which we have actually seen, those which we have seen recently enough to remember accurately, and those we have not seen at all. There is more hearsay—or seesay—in movie criticism than in any other subject outside the Vietnam War.

I am not convinced that chronology is a good concept for organizing a course in film. Pudovkin's *Mother,* like good malt whisky, is an acquired taste. It's quite possible that we shouldn't make it a required taste. This is what I object to with Ed Fischer's paper. I don't object to terminology. I have a degree in philosophy and enjoyed getting it and am supported by my training in philosophy more often than not, but no one in it ever asked me to begin with terms. We began with ideas, and found the terms we needed for ourselves. Thus I suggest that it is begging the question against the student's taste to cover him with concepts in the first weeks of a class. It is relevant to ask ourselves which films hold up. Why do they, and why don't others? Under what conditions do they hold up? *Ten Days That Shook the World* was marvellous when I saw it in a loft with a group of Stalinists. They knew where all the jokes were. By itself, you might have to create the setting for a class before they see what its point of view is. Or it might be better not to show it. Is an audience's taste wrong when it doesn't relish a classic? Or are we too free with the label? Is education all there is to it, or should we be prepared to speak in the past tense about a film's merit as we do of its production conditions? There is always a haunting feeling that to do so means that we are missing something, the most important essence of cinema, but this is an occupational hazard and you can learn to live with ignorance. For the truth is that all the facts are not in yet.

Likewise I question Arthur Knight's theory that film students should see a lot of history before they make the same old mistakes again. In our own school (U.C.L.A.), we let the students decide, even and especially the film makers, *when* they will take the history classes. But we require them to take four terms of it while they are there. I once asked a good film student when he took his history courses, and he replied that he had taken Hugh Gray's course four times now. I was reminded of Maupassant who wrote that the best time to fish is before, during, or after rain. But if you arrange a student's sequence of courses, how is he going to do when he's on his own with his camera? You have to convince me that there is any necessary moral, intellectual, or aesthetic connection between discovery and proof, between the understanding of what someone else has done, well or badly, and what you will do yourself in a creative situation.

Now this question worries me because our curriculum tries to produce film makers as well as historians. But it is also relevant for those of you who are thinking of the one course or the two courses in film study which might exist in isolation in your curricula—

whether in English or drama or radio or communications or physical education departments. In that case consider the first piece of advice given David Stewart by one of my colleagues when he first came to see us two years ago: try to have two courses, not one, and make one of them a project course, in which the students make 8-mm. movies. Buy two 8-mm. cameras, and make the students purchase their own film. Find two small viewers and splicing blocks. Give them no lectures on technique at all, but have some sympathetic, resilient colleagues screen the results with you and your class. Make this, even, a quiz section of your own class. Be comforted by the fact that U.C.L.A. currently [1965] requires twenty-three units of prerequisites for its workshop program, but next year will require no prerequisites at all.

In this second part I wish to make some suggestions that I hope we can all agree upon. I shall assume that we *are* going to get an American Film Institute.

The main ingredient I found missing in most of the papers was pessimism. The authors were all too optimistic. Having solved their own problems, they tended to conceal the tasks of scholarship which face us, and to give us a sanguine impression of satisfaction with the status quo. At other times we are prepared to admit that film scholarship in this country is in a mess.

For its Spring 1963 issue, *Film Quarterly* asked Jerzy Toeplitz, rector of the Polish Film Academy, to survey the general needs of film scholarship.[1] His analysis is still germane, and should be studied by anyone seriously interested in making a contribution to *film* scholarship, and not just fiddling around with film as art, film as poetry, film as wall paintings, and so on.

In the course of his article, Toeplitz made a very simple suggestion. Whenever any of us, or any institution with which we are connected, is engaged in or completes a piece of research, there should be a way to record and report this fact. We are all too poor

[1] Pp. 27–37.

to circulate the information, but a bulletin could do it for us. This is a job for the American Film Institute (A.F.I.). Beyond this, we must have ways to question, as Mr. Toeplitz does not, the value of the work performed. Only if we have discussion of standards, can the good be usefully separated from the bad. The A.F.I. should consider which publications it could usefully support and undertake.

When he transferred the Library of Congress paper collection to acetate, Kemp Niver drew off catalogue information which had not existed before, about each film. California is going to publish a small part of this work. Who will publish the remainder? It would not actually make a trade book, but the information should be accessible somewhere. Credits, production date, summary of review information, synopses, should be attempted for every film which is being preserved. This should be maintained as a permanent catalogue, and the information, including availability of the film, should be available to all subscribers to the catalogue. The subscription fee could not cover the costs of maintaining the catalogue, but costs could be reduced by computer storage, and the remainder carried as a service expense of the A.F.I. It would not be difficult to assemble and make accessible vast amounts of information which is currently the possession of a favored few. The Library of Congress card files could be incorporated into the catalogue; perhaps the archives would cooperate, at least to the extent that they can admit their holdings. The British Film Institute (B.F.I.) offered to make available its entire research library, if the A.F.I. would cover the out-of-pocket costs of duplication. This offer was made to me in 1962, and was matched immediately by the Belgian Cinémathèque and the Polish Academy of the Arts. Their willingness to do so indicated not only extraordinary generosity, but also an almost weary impatience to have something established in this country which they could reliably go to for help.

Surprisingly, the same is often true about films in the archives. Ernest Lindgren told me in 1962, and repeated the offer to a colleague this year, that he would make printing material available for films if A.F.I. could pay the costs of the prints. I suggested a shared use of any resulting prints, in order to recognize the costs which the B.F.I. had already incurred in preserving the film. It would be left to us to satisfy copyright owners of our intentions. At the time of the A.F.I. proposal, we had not anticipated the need for another archive in this country, but we were assuming that the Hollywood Museum would by now have been a functioning reality, instead of collecting film without really being there. But the archival matter may have to be looked at again in the light of current problems, both national and international. Perhaps I am being provincial in worrying about this, since the West has four film schools dotted along its coast, and has no archive to turn to. We must consider what an advisory group of film researchers, meeting with the archivists and representatives from the industry, could jointly accomplish in the areas of film preservation and, equally important, film restoration. I am hopeful that U.C.L.A. will soon be in a position to contribute to the restoration program, but this must become a national, not a regional concern. We should also find ways of advising the Library of Congress about its acquisition program. These also are areas of responsibility for an A.F.I.—establishing an archive in the West, another in the Midwest, and advising on their management and policies.

The A.F.I. would also be valuable in that it could function as a research institute directly, not only having advisory responsibilities. We must put the control where the action is, and the A.F.I. can provide a focus for this action best by being engaged in it. If the A.F.I. were properly constituted, with the appropriate credentials, authority, and financing, universities could join as sustaining members, and pay a fee for services, thus avoiding the need to have archives as they currently have libraries for other disciplines. We might also then be in a position to have meaningful exchanges with European archives—just by arranging that commercial prints, after use, could be deposited abroad with a national archive. That is the least we might try to arrange.

The major problem is fear of piracy—making illegal use of prints, and illegal copies. If you have a rare film, the temptation is almost irresistible to copy it. If you come by a film, which cannot be traced to you, you are tempted to keep it. The film is thus preserved, but rarely if ever used. What we need are public collections, publicly catalogued, and available to accredited scholars or schools. Perhaps it would be possible to devise a way of marking the picture area of a film so that it can be discerned when the film is examined under certain light conditions, but not others—not under projection conditions, surely. If films could be marked in this way, such that the mark inevitably passed on to a print made of it, film poaching could be controlled. It would also be worth exploring the legal requirements of proving lawful ownership of a print. Unless we do this, and even if we do, we still must enlist the aid of the Motion Picture Association of America, the Academy, the White House, and so on before the acquisition, preservation, and circulation program of an A.F.I. will even approach the thoroughness which is called for.

For archival purposes, films should at least be available in regional centers—close to the places where scholars live and must work. Scholars are prepared to move about, of course. I do not think we should object if certain cities are designated as being able to support an archive so that scholars, it is assumed, would cluster around these cities if they were not there already.

We ought to ask ourselves why there are no good books on film aesthetics in English. Is that a sign of our wisdom or our ignorance? It is probably not irrelevant that our politics is not methodical, systematic, or in the true sense of the word, dogmatic. We are more like the Scandinavians than the French or Italians in this regard, and we find that it is only the French and the Italians, and some of the Socialist nations, which have produced and continue to produce theoretical writing of any substance on the movies. Toeplitz argues that without theory an art cannot advance, and artists are tied to tradition. The French experience suggests there may be a connection between time spent as critics and work produced as film makers later, but I wonder if this is a good model for wishy-washy American liberals.

I question Toeplitz' argument that we need textbooks on direction and so on. My training in philosophy makes me sympathetic to the connection, but my experience as a film maker, teacher, and critic makes me wonder. But someone should work on this. Karel Reisz's book on editing works. It should not have to be solitary. If A.F.I. were a research center, then perhaps it could provide a home for professors on sabbatical, and help support scholars not associated with universities—presumably in collaboration with the foundations.

With the level of university commitment to film teaching which already exists in this country, it is nothing short of bewildering that so little original film scholarship is done in this country. This is a problem for all of us. Perhaps the A.F.I. can bring us together.

IT'S ONLY A MOVIE

by Pauline Kael

I SEE MOVIES, talk about them, and write about them all the time; why should it be so enervating even to consider sitting down and formulating my general approach in terms of a course? Although I accepted this commitment in good faith, I found myself postponing its accomplishment. When I could no longer put off this oppressive assignment, I sat down and looked at the original letter with its suggestions for what the paper might include: the "rationale" of the course, a description of what you hope students will gain by studying the subject with you; the sequential treatment of subjects within the course; a complete list of all texts, journals, and periodicals used in the course; a complete list of all films screened; and so on. And suddenly I heard a teenage voice inside me muttering, "Do they want the questions the students will ask, too? So you can prepare the answers in advance?"

All the hostility toward the project that I had been trying to keep down, rose to the surface. This was what I had gotten interested in movies to get away from. And I recognized the symptoms

---

PAULINE KAEL, one of America's foremost motion picture critics, writes for a variety of magazines including *The Atlantic, The New York Times Book Review, Film Quarterly, Life, Holiday,* and *McCall's.* She received a Guggenheim Fellowship in 1964 and in 1965 published a collection of essays entitled *I Lost it At the Movies.* She has lectured at colleges and universities throughout the country.

of fatigue. I remembered how my thumbnails got worn down from scraping the paint off my pencils as the teacher droned on about great literature. I remembered music appreciation with the record being played over and over, the needle arm going back and forth, and I remembered the slide machine in art history and the deadly rhythm of the instructor's tapper. And I knew that I could not present a course of study. I began to see that the reason I dreaded it, the reason I couldn't just toss it off is because I don't *believe* in it. More than that, it goes against the grain of everything I feel about movies, and against the grain of just about everything I believe about how we learn in the arts.

Perhaps you once shared my association of courses of study with institutional lethargy. Perhaps, even *most* of us got interested in movies to get away from that. And maybe the only way we can save movies from being dehydrated like other arts converted into academic "disciplines" is to consider what they meant to us earlier in our lives, what they may mean to students now, and the more terrible question of how our interests have shifted from our earlier ones and from those of students now. Possibly our personal commitments—professional, economic, institutional, or whatever—and our personal needs for career or status or success or whatever, may have caused not only an alteration in our original desires and intentions toward movies, but also they may prevent us from recognizing what students think about and want.

Let me give a simple example of the kind of shift I mean. Many film teachers got interested in movies as a vehicle of social change. Those, especially, who got involved in documentary production in the thirties and forties and from thence into teaching, were dedicated to documentary as a criticism of social and economic life. Now they train students to glorify that life, and instead of recognizing, facing, discussing these alterations in the uses of documentary, they usually find it easier to talk about training and technique, about good and bad ways of doing things. But surely the important question is: what are we doing? For if our belief in documentary film as an important force for good, for opening people's eyes to their environment and its problems, results in nothing more than helping to produce better institutional ads for Bell Telephone, then perhaps we should re-examine the nature of our beliefs. Should we go on pretending to do one thing, when the evidence shows we're doing something else?

We all know that the reason so many documentary people have become integrated into big business is that this is the only way they could practice their trade. This is something that must come out into the open if they are to give students any clear notion of how movies work in the world; and perhaps the students will respond to the facts of the situation with more alertness and interest than to the standard sentimental liberal version of documentary, its greatness, its classics, and all the rest of the fairy tale teachers cling to. Perhaps they will find ways of coping with what, for an earlier generation, was an impossible situation. But they've got to know the facts; or else they don't stand a chance of developing the principles or the strength necessary to develop documentary into a medium for individuals, as well as for corporations and government agencies.

This example has already led me far into certain areas of bitterness that I think many of us know only too intimately. There are many such examples. And, of course, students judge us by what we have become, not by what we had once hoped to be. Unless we are honest, they are not only doomed to repeat our failures, worse, they may not even develop the idealism that made us try. I have not raised such basic questions without the hope that they may lead to some fairly basic clarifications. I think we must try to remember what we once knew, as well as what we know now.

People who just enjoy movies or think they are a worthwhile subject that should be taught, do not know or understand what movies do to those who have the misfortune to fall in love with this mass medium—a medium which seems almost inevitably to break the hearts of those who really care about it.

One might even formulate it—the more you care, the more it destroys you; the more you refuse to compromise, to betray your love, the less you can do. The documentarian who doesn't work for a big corporation, or for a school training kids to work for big corporations, doesn't work. The Hollywood director who spent his youth on venal projects in the hope that once he had a reputation he could do something he cared about, usually finds himself working on bigger venal projects, or not working at all.

The "successful" directors are unlikely to have much love left, except by turning it on themselves; the astonishing ego of directors who carry on in the flamboyant genius tradition may be a necessary mechanism for their survival in the industry. For you must not only be terribly tough and calculating and shrewd to make movies (or to direct plays, for that matter), you must also be able to convince others and possibly even yourself that what you're doing is a work of genius and art; you must very nearly sell the idea that you're the center of the world. And generally you have to be a little crazy to sell this. If you aren't a brilliant paranoiac, then it may help to be a charlatan. Usually they're a little of both. Talented frauds survive the longest.

All this is what educators and those who want a sensible, intelligent incorporation of good film into the curriculum are not going to understand or be able to believe; if they did, it would disturb their role as educators. Perhaps you can't understand it unless you're enough involved in movies to experience it, and if so, it's too late. You're already partly sunk in the quicksand, in those fantasies that sustain hope, the fantasies that somehow the course of movie history will be reversed, that the talented people will get a chance to do what they want, that large audiences will be won over to good work, that independent production, or new methods of distribution, or a film institute or government funds or even a new department head, will make a crucial difference. (I have learned when talking with movie directors never to ask what happened to the project they were just about to start the last time I spoke with them. In one form or another, everyone connected with movies seems to spend most of his life and almost all of his energy on projects that are never realized.)

Recently I read Lionel Trilling's "Reflections on the Study of English."[1] As he discussed the environments for the study of literature in such calm, measured phrases as "adherence to the imagination of fullness, freedom, and potency of life" and "firm presuppositions, received ideas, approved attitudes, and a system of rewards and punishments," I was impressed with the beautiful serenity of this vision of formulating clear thoughts, writing usefully, leading a civilized life; I was also horrified and amused at the distance from our common life that it takes for granted. Those of us in movies don't have this distance; I hope we don't get it. For if we do, it means that movies have lost the vitality that drew us to them, or that *we* have lost it. I wondered, reading Trilling, if there was any way even for those engaged in teaching in the other arts to understand the desperation of their colleagues teaching film.

If I may use an analogy to illustrate this chasm: in a recent article, Jim Collier contrasted the day to day life of Roger Stevens, head of the National Council of the Arts, and an American artist who lives just a few blocks from him, Thelonius Monk. For example, while Monk, busted by the police, had lost his cabaret card and couldn't work, Stevens bought the Empire State Building. Collier concludes that: "Although Roger Stevens and Thelonius Monk walk the same streets of the same city, hear the same sounds, perhaps even drink the same brand of Scotch, they inhabit environments so removed from each other, and have passed through lives so unrelated, that it is impossible that either could ever understand the other."

Movie people are closer to jazzmen than to academics and cultural bureaucrats who have been protected in ways that we are

[1] *Encounter,* July 1965.

not. Our sense of the world is different from theirs. They want to talk about art and culture-explosions and standards and improving taste and all the rest of it, and we are obsessed with a rotten world of business, a corrupted art, and pressures toward conformity and tastelessness that have destroyed the hopes of all idealists. Even the small hopes of cynics are destroyed by movies.

How can we expect university or teaching colleagues who have a polite appreciative interest in movies to understand what it took those of us trapped in movies a long time to learn, and what the new students who are so caught up in the excitement of becoming "film makers"—that extraordinary term which already points to the egomania necessary for survival in the film world—have so little awareness of? We didn't know what we were getting into either.

We were—and I am, of course, only guessing about you—driven to the movies as a compensatory necessity—a flight, and I don't mean a mere escape, to a world more exciting than the deadening world of trying-to-be-helpful teachers and chewed-over texts. We were driven to it by our own energies, which were not sufficiently engaged, not imaginatively used in the rest of our lives. We wanted more and we got it, or at least gorgeous hints of it, at the movies.

If, in earlier periods, the child laborer fled to the library, trying to expand his world, we, as school children, similarly fled to the movies. It is not necessarily an escape into fantasy, any more than reading novels or essays or history is; it may just as easily, more easily, be interpreted as a flight from routine and complacence and uninvolvement into—what? Intensity, perhaps, and complexity, and pleasure, and frustration.

Movies turn into something else when you get close to them—like those firecrackers that look like candies until you bite on them and part of your head gets torn off. With movies it takes a while for that to happen.

We go to movies because we want to. That's the big thing and the starting point for any discussion. The greatest advantage movies had for us and still have, the great advantage of film over the other arts, is that it has *not* been forced on us. It has been ours like jazz and popular music—something we wanted, not something fed to us. With, no doubt, the best intentions in the world, poetry, classical music, even painting, sculpture, and architecture, were forced on us, and thus we were deprived of them. As T. E. Lawrence said, "Either forced evil or forced good will make a people cry out in pain."

There has been a great deal of speculation about why movies have become a religion to this generation, and I think there may be two parts to the answer.

The first, and it was true for earlier generations too, is that in the terms children experience them, motion pictures have remained so free. They are almost the only free province left (if by movies we include television film also), free, that is, of adult encouragement, interpretation, pushing. Surely only social deviates would say to a child, "What's the matter with you, why don't you want to go to the movies?" Kids don't have to get all dressed up or go with an adult the way they do to a Leonard Bernstein concert, shiny and flushed with the privilege of being there. No cultural glow suffuses the Saturday afternoon movie audience; they are still free to react as *they* feel like reacting, with derision or excitement or disappointment or whatever. Nobody says you have to like a movie (not, that is, until you get to the art-house age) and, as it isn't an occasion, there's no aftermath for you to fear. Going to a movie doesn't wind up with the horrors of reprimands for your restlessness, with nervous reactions, tears, and family disappointments that you weren't up to it. It's only a movie. What beautiful words. At the movies, you're left gloriously alone. You can say it stinks and nobody's shocked. That's something you can't do with a Dickens novel or a Beethoven symphony or even a poem by Browning, and because you can't, because they're all preselected and prejudged and graded for greatness, you don't talk about them with the other kids the way you do about movies.

The second part—*why* the new religion of film is more complex. It's related to our times and the peculiarities of our times. I think—although there are some terrors in this thinking—that teenagers and college-age people may be caught up in movies because movies are a medium in which it's possible to respond in such an infinity of ways to an infinity of material without forming precise or definite attitudes, or making conscious judgments, or referring to values of any kind beyond "cinema," as if the medium were an end in itself.

This, I think, may help to explain their enthusiasm for certain particularly mindless commercial directors as well as for a number of art films whose meanings and implications don't seem to interest them. They don't ask *why* of a movie; they seem to accept what goes on in it as if it were a fact of nature. "That's just how the man felt like doing it," they'll say, as if that were sufficient. And for them it seems to be. By "art" they mean whatever a person felt like expressing, and because it is his personal expression they regard it as beyond criticism. (Let us agree, in passing, that criticism and teaching are basically the same function. The critic uses the writer's medium; the teacher works more directly with those to be influenced in personal contact. Our responsibilities are the same.)

If only they had concealed their enthusiasm for movies! Now that it's out in the open it's too big to be left to them. They've created what may be their own Frankenstein monster: us. The big push is on.

Although everyone who wants to know knows that much of the pressure to introduce motion-picture study into American schools is from the motion-picture industry, there is great and widespread enthusiasm and the usual hopes that "educated" audiences will want "mature" films. Within the industry there is even talk that young moviegoers who have been defecting to foreign films will be won back if they are educated to our American movie heritage. An extraordinary assumption, but then, these are desperate men. They see all those spontaneously generated kids now showing up in the population statistics—and population statistics are only folding money away from box-office figures. The industry wants to attract young dollars, and if a new generation is interested in the art of the film, the industry will do anything to please for a profit. The kids want "underground movies"; the industry will supply them. Certainly they'll be only too happy to encourage teachers to understand how artistic American movies are. Do they really imagine that educated moviegoers will prefer *their* movies? It may be a long shot but it's not costing them anything. The government pays for education.

There are so many ways for us to go wrong. I think the most basic way, the standard way is the worst. I refer, of course, to the Pollyanna-type appreciation course showing the history of film as a steady march of creativity ending with colleges recognizing the newest art. It's very like those movie biographies of the lives of the great in which the climax of the life is obviously the film itself.

I suppose an inspired teacher could make even this course work, and yet, if you will forgive me, I doubt if he could stay inspired doing it over and over again. And from the way these courses sound, even hearing them described briefly, doesn't a terrible fatigue set in—some small indication of how the students must react week after week?

Why not use the student's current interests to lead them into the past? We don't have to worry if it's a little disorderly; in this field gaps of knowledge are not criminal negligence as they might be for a doctor.

It would probably be a disaster to talk about *Ivan the Terrible* the week the students were excited about *Alphaville.* But if we're flexible enough, we could use *Alphaville* as a springboard to Méliès and *Things to Come* and *Metropolis;* it's easy to get from Rotwang to Strangelove to any place we want to go. Almost any TV commercials can lead into Eisenstein, or working in a different direction, into Richard Lester. The James Bond movies can take us to the early serials; we can deflate *The Ipcress File* by going to *The Maltese Falcon;* almost any modern comedy can lead into Preston

Sturges or Howard Hawks. The airport of *The Married Woman* is not only derived from but can point to *The Rules of the Game.* The newspaper headline *Je vous dit merde* of *Jules and Jim* is not only a quote from *Zero for Conduct,* but has enough historical ramifications to open up all of French movie history. Or we can go from the bed of *The Knack* to the barge of *L'Atalante.*

There is so much that students don't know about that you do; can't this be drawn upon as it is relevant, rather than fed to students when they have no appetite for it?

And there's enough that's surprising in *their* reactions to keep *you* going, if you give them a chance to open up. For example, why they react to the spirit of *What's New, Pussycat?,* why they accept the arbitrariness of Godard, the doldrums of Antonioni. If we don't get this from them *right at the time* they feel it, we lose touch. And if we don't connect with them, they're not going to connect with us. And we're all in the blackboard jungle of stale subjects.

I know you're not going to fight the movement of educational institutions into movies, you're going to join it. In fact, you intend to lead it.

My purpose here is, hopefully, to prevent our doing more damage than is absolutely necessary. From what I've said in general, a few small suggestions and ideas may perhaps follow. Even if you reject everything I've said so far, you still might go along with me on some of these points. They're not in any rational sequence or in any order except as they happened to occur to me as I was putting them down. I'll use the term "you" rather than "we" simply in order to hit you harder.

1. It is true that if you work very hard and if the foundations and councils and associations are cooperative, you can make cinema as respectable, as full of status as other academic subjects. *Don't.* Because you can only do that by pretending movie content is irrele-

vant, by making cinema courses the empty study of images and sound. Respectable is what movies are not, and that's what we love about them.

2. *Use* the foundations and councils and associations; *don't* let them use you. As an example, try to get funds for people with talent, but don't let their ideas be circumscribed by institutional restrictions.

3. Don't join in the push for texts for movie courses. A reading list is probably unavoidable, possibly useful if it's voluntary, not required reading, and if you make it up considering the students' interests and needs, not your academic fence-mending and fee-splitting and prestige-position-jockeying. But in the arts, a text is a book that, under the guise of simplifying, makes things more dull and meaningless and difficult and forgettable than they have ever been. A text is like medicine: it's a book you don't want to read that is supposed to be good for you. And in the arts—and this is their glory—nothing you don't want is good for you. If *Ten Days That Shook the World* bores a student, there is no proof, no power on earth, to say he has got to like it. If a lady says, "That man don't pleasure me," that's it. There are some areas in which we can decide for ourselves.

But teachers don't let us decide for ourselves: they'll set up a neat batch of masterpieces for awed appreciation, and they can turn *Singin' in the Rain* into *Idylls of the King*. Stanza by stanza. Not understanding a movie never ruined anybody's life, but proper, informed, educated opinions are like paralysis. When you've got it, you don't want much else.

4. If you think movies can't be killed, you underestimate the power of education. Don't make students look at films over and over again. I have never been able to forget the stricken look on my daughter's face when she came home from her progressive kindergarten after two showings of Pare Lorentz' *The River;* appar-

ently the children hadn't paid sufficient attention the first time, so the teacher made them look at it again.

If they're bored the first time, it can only get worse. Don't make them hate *all* movies because *you* picked the wrong movie at the wrong time.

The new textbook, *The Motion Picture and the Teaching of English,* financed by a grant from Teaching Film Custodians, a branch of the Motion Picture Association, to the National Council of Teachers of English—that shows which way the important winds are blowing, doesn't it?—includes remarks like: "Such film criticism as that of Otis Ferguson and Dwight Macdonald and Stanley Kauffmann requires more than one seeing of a film. . . ."[2] It's the rare movie that critics see more than once: this mania for repeated viewings is, in different form, that old dreadnought, the paraphrase. Surely a second viewing should always be voluntary, determined by the individual's further interests. If the dull ones didn't get it the first time, don't go back; pass on. Maybe sometime later they'll respond to it, maybe not. Insistence, nagging kill pleasure.

Don't embalm movies with all this obsequious attention; if you're going to kill them, have the decency not to linger over your victim.

5. If honest advice is not enough to deter you from envisioning writing brilliant texts, here, as a footnote on academic scholarship, are some particularly interesting movies discussed in *The Motion Picture and the Teaching of English:* Kurosawa's *Gate of Hell,* Delbert Mann's *The Mark,* William Wyler's *The Lost Weekend.* (I hope I don't need to tell you that the films were directed by Kinugasa, Guy Green, and Billy Wilder.) I hope you don't think I'm pointing this out just to be bitchy. My point is that already in this text for training teachers to teach motion picture in the high schools, the authors use the directors' names as a ritual gesture. Which indicates that it will soon be incumbent on high school students to refer to movies with the directors' names attached, even if those names mean nothing to them, as indeed they probably mean

[2] Marion C. Sheridan *et al., The Motion Picture and the Teaching of English* (New York: Appleton-Century-Crofts, 1965), p. 137.

very little to the authors if they could ascribe *Gate of Hell* to Kurosawa, *The Mark* to Delbert Mann, and *The Lost Weekend* to William Wyler. Can't you already see the hatred building up with students who say something about *Earth* or *Greed* and are then put down by the teacher saying, "We don't refer to movies as if they were anonymous. Now who directed *Earth* and *Greed?* That's right, we say, Dovzhenko's *Earth* and Von Stroheim's *Greed.*" But, of course, as the teachers are new at this game, there'll probably be years of Eisenstein's *Earth* and Von Sternberg's *Greed* before they get all this empty ornamentation of culture memorized right. But when they do, it will give them great cultural superiority over those mass-audience clucks who don't care who made the movie. This may be just about all they'll get out of it.

This textbook is so loaded with status and credentials it might as well invent its own data. It has a production team of a project director, a chief writer, two associate writers, plus two liaison officers; and there are several pages of thank-yous to people who helped or read the manuscript or suggested something or other. It is, in other words, a product of artificial insemination, one assumes well-lubricated. No wonder it reads like a text. Don't assume yours will be better because it will be different.

We all know that if texts exist, *somebody's* going to use them. It's so easy, it's irresistible. Many of you already use texts that are safe because they're devoid of obvious personal opinion, personal judgments, personal feelings, personal responses. This is supposed to make them objective. The author is frequently a team—a more fashionable new academic method of authorship which also has the practical advantage of ensuring adoption in a group of schools; or he is an individual who writes like a team, careful to be impersonal, not to give offense, to rephrase all the tired accepted opinions of the nonentities who preceded him. He will show his open-mindedness by including mention of people and topics his predecessors didn't approve of that can no longer be ignored.

Of course, yours is going to be a *good* text, but when educators talk firmly and solemnly about good texts it's like TV executives talking about a good series. After a while taste deteriorates: the less bad begins to be considered great. Those who aren't familiar with the average are appalled when they see the best.

In the arts, a good text doesn't mean a good book. Books are written by writers; texts are written by people in strategic institutional positions. Texts are probably indispensable in fields where technical material can be reduced. But they have almost no place in an art which is not codified, where taste varies, and where there is no such thing as final authority or absolute standards—even of what is now called "excellence."

6. Isn't the fantastic new interest in movies—bad as they now are, and they are excruciatingly bad at the moment—evidence in itself that students are turning to movies because they seem alive compared with the other arts? And if movies, the remnants of the art of movies, after over sixty years of commercial exploitation and the degradation of being bound to mass consumption patterns, still have more life and excitement and promise than the other arts, then isn't there a pretty strong chance that exclusion from official culture has had something to do with this vitality and survival?

Even those of you who may agree about what will happen to movies when they are taught will probably say that it's a shame, but it's inevitable, it's a necessary stage and it must be gone through. I wish I could be sure something will come out the other end. It's possible that the institutional clamp-down on movies will seal off the last major terrain, leaving only the thin strip of popular music and the heavily trod alley of folk singing and no place to go but that region of the mind already being explored by so many students and underground film makers, their own mushroom cloud.

7. There is a possibility, but it will rub against many of your career interests—for, of course, at last you are about to cash in, to be somebody, your field has been discovered, important people consult you, your advice suddenly *counts.* Are you likely, at this stage, the consummation of so many almost-buried desires, to con-

sider jumping over the respectable teaching stage, jumping right into what is now being attempted in the other arts, trying new methods of applying oxygen not on a corpse, but on those still eager to breathe, those who want more air.

Bring in for discussions, for film showings, for lectures, for a night or a week or a month or a term, the movie equivalent of artists-in-residence. *Not* just the great men, the sensitive men, and the frustrated talents, but the hardened commercial hacks, the gravel-voiced producers, the ferrety agents, the sentimental, self-righteous blacklisted writers, the directors who have never made a competent movie, the exploitation film makers who didn't even try, the cutters who couldn't get into the butchers' union, the dubbers and all the rest; the critics who have always panned the great ones, and the blackmailing gossip columnists, and the union bosses, and the old stars who will do anything to appear on television as celebrities. Let them show their wares and explain the whys and hows of the movie business. Invite the snotty young and not so young experimenters, not just the talented ones and the honest ones, but the pretentious, arrogant little bastards with their fifty-five ways of explaining the greatness of the blur on the screen. They lie about art but they do know something about show business. Show your students the big money makers, the all-time top-grossers, those huge displays of whoremongering and tastelessness and condescension that are enjoyed by people all over the world, and maybe they'll begin to understand something of what makes movies an impossible heart breaking near-possibility. Maybe they'll begin to see how it all works. They'll learn something about motion-picture business.

This won't be respectable: motion picture will not be admitted to the curriculum as a newly recognized, full-fledged, or, as the institution may decide, fledgling art. Your status might even be jeopardized. But that's such a small price to pay.

8. Another hope for students is that there might be some film nuts among their teachers. Those of us who were lucky in our edu-

cations had perhaps one or two genuine eccentrics: perhaps a squat little old lady who wore the same oatmeal suit all semester and recited Greek to us when she couldn't stand the history text any longer; or a skinny woman with spiky hairs on her chin and a chestnut-colored wig, a woman whose eyes would glaze with fervor as she intoned poetry. Maybe it wasn't even good poetry; for that matter, we didn't even need to understand the Greek. What mattered was that they cared, they loved it, and we felt their love. Maybe their passion was a little embarrassing; and not just in class. Probably some people who saw them on the street poked each other and smiled. Did that matter?

We can all at least take it this far: don't talk about movies you don't care about one way or another. Concentrate on movies you love or hate, or your indifference will infect your students. Don't discuss a movie just because it's a classic or a milestone.

9. As we are all aware, colleges love to justify showing movies for fun and profit by referring to them as classics and masterpieces. Wherever possible, discourage this practice. This academic version of the hard-sell is already inflating the reputation of a number of fairly good and some pretty awful movies that happen to be easily available or appealing to whoever happens to do the booking. The phony classics come-on is much more dishonest than the sex come-on used by regular theaters. Its purpose is obviously hypocritical—disguising commercial intentions with high-sounding explanations. There is enough of this in the world; let's not add to it.

And, in connection with this, *don't* try to justify movies you show that your students don't like by clobbering the students with the information that these are recognized, acknowledged classics, among the greatest movies of all time, etc. If you flop, you flop. Learn to live with it. You'll probably feel that it's *you* more than the film that they're rejecting, and you may be right, but it doesn't help to pull rank—whether yours or the film's—on them.

10. The individual with hints of talent and outrageously large

demands will be a tantalizing problem and ultimately a nuisance to you. He'll come to you now as he used to batter at the doors of the industry. It will be easier for him to get at you and he'll be maddening. He'll treat *you* as the establishment and you're not used to that yet. Chances are he'll be sullen on pot, withdrawn and contemptuous of you, and you'll decide he's impossible, he just won't adapt and there's nothing you can do about it. *Try.*

11. If you're easily corrupted, you'll be charmed to discover how the industry now respects you. You'll discover how they're changing. Why they're at least as civilized as you are. Hollywood is becoming so modulated in tone and so cleverly groomed and costumed that it could almost pass for the academic-institutional-foundation world. I had lunch in the executive dining room at one of the studios recently and the men around me looked like Ivy League New Frontiersmen. I wouldn't have known I was in a studio except that they looked around nervously every time I cracked a joke.

Industry people will hope you're some kind of new magician who knows what's happening. You'll probably feel guilty if you advise them on how to "grab" the younger generation. But your feelings of guilt will be mere self-indulgence because your advice will no doubt be out-dated by the time they act on it anyway. This will permit you the luxury of feeling that you were true to your principles and deliberately out-witted them.

12. To close on a semi-hopeful note:

For reasons which seem to be rooted in the aesthetics of their formative years, a great many film people seem to think they must devote their thinking to discovering the true, essential nature of cinema, so that they can certify cinema as a pure field with laws, principles, boundaries.

Isn't it clear that trying to find out what cinema "really" is, is derived from a mad Platonic and metaphorical view of the universe—as if ideal, pure cinema were some pre-existent entity that we had to find? Cinema is not to be found; but movies are continuously being made. And with the loss of interest in other arts, perhaps we can even help to extend what movies can do into fields that were previously thought to be the domain of journalists, painters, poets, novelists, essayists, dramatists, scientists, whatever.

APPENDIXES

APPENDIX A

Film Distributors

American Cinema Editors
8741 Sunset Boulevard
Los Angeles 69, California

Audio Film Center
2138 East 75th Street
Chicago 49, Illinois

406 Clement Street
San Francisco 18, California

10 Fiske Place
Mount Vernon, New York

Brandon Films, Inc.
200 West 57th Street
New York 19, New York

Carousel Films
450 West 56th Street
New York, New York

Center for Mass Communication
Columbia University
1125 Amsterdam Avenue
New York, New York

Cinema 16
175 Lexington Avenue
New York 16, New York

Contemporary Films
267 West 25th Street
New York 1, New York

614 Davis Street
Evanston, Illinois

1211 Polk Street
San Francisco 9, California

Creative Film Society
14558 Valerio Street
Van Nuys, California

DuArt Film Labs.
245 West 55th Street
New York 19, New York

Embassy 16mm
Time-Life Building
Rockefeller Center
New York 20, New York

Encyclopaedia Britannica Films
See Films Incorporated

Film Center, Inc.
20 East Huron Street
Chicago 11, Illinois

Film Images
See Radim Films, Inc.

Films Incorporated
1150 Wilmette Avenue
Wilmette, Illinois

Film-Makers Cooperative
414 Park Avenue South
New York 16, New York

Ideal Pictures, Inc.
58 East South Water Street
Chicago, Illinois
(about 10 branch offices)

Indiana University
Audio Visual Center
Bloomington, Indiana

Janus Film Library
Hotel Wellington
55th Street and 7th Avenue
New York 19, New York

McGraw-Hill Publishing Co.
Text-Films Division
330 West 42nd Street
New York 36, New York

Museum of Modern Art Film Library
11 West 53rd Street
New York 19, New York

Northwestern University
Department of Communicative Disorders
School of Speech
Evanston, Illinois 60201

N.Y.U. Film Library
26 Washington Place
New York, New York

OFM Productions
1229 South Santee Street
Los Angeles, California

Prudential Insurance Co.
(Contact local offices)

Radim Films, Inc.
220 West 42nd Street
New York 36, New York

Reade-Sterling
241 East 34th Street
New York, New York

Rehabilitation Institute of Chicago
401 East Ohio Street
Chicago 11, Illinois

Royal 16 International
711 Fifth Avenue
New York 22, New York

Trans-World Films
332 South Michigan Avenue
Room 528 McCormick Building
Chicago 4, Illinois

Twyman Films
329 Salem Avenue
Dayton, Ohio

United Charities of Chicago
123 West Madison Street
Chicago, Illinois 60602

United States Information Agency*
Motion Picture Service
1776 Pennsylvania Avenue, N.W.
Washington, D.C. 20547

United World Films
287 Techwood Drive, N.W.
Atlanta, Georgia

542 South Dearborn Street
Chicago 5, Illinois

2227 Bryan Street
Dallas 1, Texas

7374 Melrose Avenue
Los Angeles 46, California

105 East 106th Street
New York 29, New York

5023 N.E. Sandy Boulevard
Portland 13, Oregon

University of California
Motion Picture Division
University Extension
Berkeley 4, California

University of Southern California
Film Library, Department of Cinema
University Park
Los Angeles 7, California

University of Wisconsin
Film Library
Madison, Wisconsin

Westinghouse Electric Corporation
Appliance Sales
6500 West Cortland
Chicago, Illinois

* Except for *Years of Lightning, Day of Drums,* USIA films are produced only for use in foreign countries.

The United States Office of Education has prepared a 532-page document entitled *U.S. Government Films for Public Educational Use—1963,* which contains a subject index as well as an alphabetical listing of titles. It sells for $3.00 and may be obtained from the Superintendent of Documents, U.S. Government Printing Office, Washington, D.C. 20402.

APPENDIX B

Professional Associations

AMERICAN FEDERATION OF FILM SOCIETIES
144 Bleecker Street
New York, New York 10012

William A. Starr, *Executive Secretary*

The American Federation of Film Societies is an incorporated nonprofit educational and cultural membership organization established to assist and advance the film society movement in the United States. Its expanding membership now numbers over five hundred active member organizations, most of them colleges, schools, and universities.

The purposes of the federation are related exclusively to the exhibition and study of film for serious purpose as a medium of education, communication, and art.

Staff officers of the federation are responsible to its Executive Secretary, who is appointed by the A.F.F.S. Board of Directors—these in turn being elected by the voting membership. Most working officers receive partial compensation for their services out of membership dues, which are also used to pay for the *Film Society Review* (monthly, September through May) and other publications which appear from time to time.

Membership dues are $25.00 per year for Society Affiliates and $10.00 per year for Associates. The *Film Society Review* is also available on simple subscription for $5.00 per year.

Further information may be obtained from: William A. Starr, Executive Secretary, 144 Bleecker Street, New York, New York 10012.

National Screen Education Committee
15 Trowbridge Street
Cambridge, Massachusetts

Anthony W. Hodgkinson, *Chairman*
David J. Powell, *Secretary*

"Screen Education" is the internationally accepted term for the organized development of responsive and critical film-goers and television viewers. It is the screen educator's belief that this can best be effected with children and young people, through the formal channels of education.

The movement, which began in Great Britain in 1950 with the formation of the Society for Education in Film and Television (S.E.F.T.), has now become widespread in Europe, Australia, Canada, and elsewhere, and is strongly supported by Unesco. The Unesco publication *Screen Education* (No. 42 in the series *Reports and Papers on Mass Communications*) summarizes the philosophy and practice of screen education.

N.S.E.C. is the U.S. national organization, affiliated with S.E.F.T. and distributing its publications in addition to its own U.S. newsletter. It makes possible contacts among members all over the country and provides information about the latest developments in the field.

Membership:
$9.00 per annum—with subscription to S.E.F.T.'s bi-monthly journal, *Screen Education,* and its *Screen Education Yearbook.*

$5.00 per annum—N.S.E.C. newsletter and services only.

Further information may be obtained from: David J. Powell, 15 Trowbridge Street, Cambridge, Massachusetts, or Professor A. W. Hodgkinson, Boston University, School of Public Relations and Communications, 640 Commonwealth Avenue, Boston, Massachusetts 02215.

THE SOCIETY OF CINEMATOLOGISTS
School of Public Relations and Communications
Boston University
640 Commonwealth Avenue
Boston, Massachusetts 02215

Robert Steele, *President*
John Kuiper, *Secretary*

The society is composed of college and university faculty and others concerned with the study of the moving picture as an art form. It was founded in 1959 as an outgrowth of the annual conferences of film teachers held by the Museum of Modern Art in New York City. The purpose of the society is the study of the moving image. Its membership is made up of approximately sixty persons who are teaching film or are involved in research and criticism relating to film; however, the society lists among its members film makers and distributors as well. The central focus of the society is its endeavor to be a learned society committed to the cinema.

The society publishes a *Journal* and has for the past three years administered grants to young film makers and screen playwrights on behalf of the Rosenthal Foundation.

Further information about the aims and programs of the society may be obtained from Robert Steele, Boston University, 640 Commonwealth Avenue, Boston, Massachusetts 02215.

UNIVERSITY FILM PRODUCERS ASSOCIATION
Ohio State University
1885 Neil Avenue
Columbus 10, Ohio

Robert W. Wagner, *Director of Motion Picture Division*

The University Film Producers Association was formed in 1947. Its purposes as stated in its constitution are:

1. To further and develop the potentialities of the motion-picture medium for purposes of instruction and communication throughout the world;

2. To encourage the production of motion pictures at the various educational institutions;
3. To encourage and assist those members in recognized educational institutions engaged in the teaching of the arts and sciences of motion-picture production techniques, film history, criticism, and related subjects;
4. To serve as a central source of information on film instruction and film production by educational institutions;
5. To provide means for the sharing of ideas on the various activities involved in teaching film courses and in the production and distribution of motion pictures and other recorded materials.

Its membership includes 147 active, 73 associate, and 76 sustaining.

The association publishes a quarterly *Journal,* holds an annual conference at a key university where films produced by students and staffs of members are critiqued, and is the official representative of the United States in the International Liaison Center of Schools of Cinema and TV.

Further information concerning U.F.P.A. may be obtained from Robert W. Wagner, Professor and Director, Motion Picture Division, Ohio State University, 1885 Neil Avenue, Columbus 10, Ohio.

APPENDIX C

Archives, Libraries, and Film Societies

GEORGE EASTMAN HOUSE
900 East Avenue
Rochester, New York

James Card, *Vice-Director* and *Curator of Motion Pictures*
George Pratt, *Assistant Curator of Motion Pictures*

George Eastman House opened in 1949 as a public educational institute, chartered by the State University of New York. Its activities, which emphasize the collection and exhibition of photographs, motion pictures, and photographic equipment, serve as a living memorial to George Eastman, pioneer in photography and former resident of the House.

In addition to a special collection of some fifty thousand photographs of all periods, Eastman House maintains over three thousand motion-picture films and more than one million still photographs. A book library further documents the history of motion pictures.

Associates of George Eastman House, a membership organization, receive the institute's news bulletin, *Image,* six times a year. Eastman House is financially maintained by annual grants from the Eastman Kodak Company plus membership dues.

The motion-picture study collection was begun in 1950 and is designed to enable students to:

1. examine each film which constitutes a major development in technique or style of film making;
2. observe the manner in which changing social problems affected the

motion picture and how they were in turn affected by the public's reaction to popular films;

3. trace the growth or decline in the work of leading motion-picture artists;
4. learn the major steps in the development and use of motion pictures, specialized in their purposes;
5. refer to newsreels and documentaries as source material in the study of specific events, or to obtain authentic details of dress and architecture;
6. compare the several versions of identical stories many of which have been repeated at intervals spanning most of the history of motion pictures.

These objectives have been pursued through the operation of various programs.

Films in the study collection are shown on request and without charge to anyone having a specific and serious interest in any phase of motion-picture history. A group of the films selected by area educators is shown on the premises throughout the school year to groups from the area universities, secondary and elementary schools.

The Dryden Theatre Film Society, with a large membership, meets at Eastman House for more than fifty programs each season. At these meetings, film programs are shown, also preceded by lectures concerning the history of motion pictures. The Film Society is supplemented by two special study groups: the foreign-language group concentrates on a special series of German, French, or Italian films and enables school groups working with these languages to attend the programs. The "Cinema Seminar" is a discussion group, composed of the most keenly interested members of the Film Society, which meets once a month to view films of highly limited interest or esoteric nature.

Supplementing the collection of historical motion pictures, Eastman House maintains the world's largest collection of motion-picture cameras, projectors, and associated equipment. Many of the early cameras and projectors are on display and mechanized so that by pressing a button, visitors can examine the operation of the various types of intermittent movements characterizing these devices.

A college credit course, "The History and Aesthetics of Photography and Motion Pictures" is taught at Eastman House for students of the Rochester Institute of Technology by Beaumont Newhall (Director of Eastman House) and by James Card (Vice-Director). A course in "History and Aesthetics of Cinema" is scheduled to be taught by James Card at Syracuse University in 1966.

THE LIBRARY OF CONGRESS
Motion Picture Section
Prints and Photographs Division
Washington, D.C.

John B. Kuiper, *Head*

The motion-picture collection of the Library of Congress is large and unique in many respects. Although the greater part of the collection is American, a large number of German, Italian, and Japanese films, captured or confiscated during World War II, have been transferred to the library by the Office of Alien Property of the Department of Justice. The collection comprises about eighty thousand reels of film and is in the custody of the Prints and Photographs Division of the Reference Department.

This extensive collection is maintained primarily for scholarly study and research. Public projection and loan services are not available but every attempt is made to provide recognized scholars, graduate students, and researchers adequate access to the collection. Copies of films which are not restricted by copyright or by the provisions of their gift or transfer to the library may be ordered through the Motion Picture Section. The section also maintains a modest reading and viewing area which contains many of the standard motion-picture reference sources as well as adequate viewing equipment.

The library's collection began in the early 1890's through the operation of the copyright law. In addition to copyright deposits, more than one thousand motion pictures have been acquired through the purchase of the George Kleine collection and through such gifts as the Ernst collection of early comedies and animated cartoons, the Allen collection of documentary and entertainment films, the Mary Pickford collection, and the Dunstan collection of William S. Hart films. Recent acquisitions by gift or transfer from other government agencies include early films from the Edison Laboratory at West Orange, New Jersey, and examples of educational television donated by N.E.T.

The Copyright Cataloging Division of the Copyright Office prepares a semiannual *Catalog of Copyright Entries: Motion Pictures and Filmstrips,* which lists all such materials registered for copyright in the United States and which is published by the library and sold by the Government Printing Office. It has also prepared four cumulative catalogs entitled *Motion Pictures* which together cover registrations of films for the years 1894–1959 and which are for sale by the Government Printing Office.

In addition, the library's Descriptive and Subject Cataloging Divisions have cataloged educational films since 1952, using data supplied largely by producers and distributors. The library publishes this catalog information in two useful forms for purchase by other libraries or by individuals. One form is the printed card, which any film-user may purchase to establish his own card catalog for the control of his collection and for the dissemination of film information. The other is a book catalog reproduced photographically from the printed cards and containing a detailed subject index, adequately cross-indexed. This book catalog, entitled *Library of Congress Catalog—Motion Pictures and Filmstrips,* is issued quarterly and in annual cumulation. It also appears as a volume in the quinquennial cumulation of the library's *National Union Catalog.* Both the printed catalog cards and the book catalog may be purchased from the Card Division, Library of Congress, Building 159, Navy Yard Annex, Washington, D.C. 20541. The book catalog is available on an annual subscription of $7.50, plus 50¢ postage.

The preservation of the motion-picture collection has been one of the prime concerns of the library since 1942. Many of the early motion pictures deposited between 1896–1912 consisted of a series of positive photographs printed on rolls of paper instead of on celluloid. They were difficult to examine and impossible to project. Furthermore, the original negatives of many of these paper positives have been lost or have deteriorated in the vaults of their producers. In 1948 the Academy of Motion Picture Arts and Sciences sponsored experiments to develop a practical method of re-photographing the paper prints onto

16-mm. safety film. After a satisfactory technique had been perfected, the academy paid for the conversion of sixteen hundred titles. Since 1958, the Congress of the United States has appropriated funds to complete the project. The preservation of this important part of the collection was completed during 1964.

Nearly one-third of the film in the collection, approximately twenty-three thousand reels, is printed on highly flammable nitrate stock which must be stored in fireproof vaults outside the District of Columbia. The library is making every effort to convert this footage to safety base stock in order to preserve it and to make reference service more efficient and convenient. The Mary Pickford collection of some two hundred titles has been converted with funds donated by Miss Pickford. Appropriated funds and income derived from the copying of unrestricted films have enabled the library to preserve several hundred pre-1920 films and to begin converting American features and newsreels dating from World War II to 1950.

THE ACADEMY OF MOTION PICTURE
ARTS AND SCIENCES
9036 Melrose Avenue
Hollywood 69, California

Mrs. Margaret Herrick, *Executive Director*

Best known for its presentation of the annual Academy Awards—the now-famous "Oscars"—the academy was founded in 1927 as a non-profit corporation. Its thirty-six charter members included production executives and film stars. Douglas Fairbanks, Sr., was its first president. It is an honorary organization composed of more than twenty-five hundred motion-picture industry craftsmen in thirteen separate branches of film making.

In addition to operating what has been described as one of the most complete collections of technical and historical information about the motion-picture industry (five thousand books and periodicals), the academy also maintains a film archive of about two thousand titles. It should be noted that the film collection is not fully representative of important historic films and that the academy has not been collecting prints for the past fifteen years. The card catalogue of films is, however, available to students, and on special request films will be screened for persons seeking information on specific titles.

THE MUSEUM OF MODERN ART
FILM LIBRARY
11 West 53rd Street
New York, New York 10019

Willard Van Dyke, *Director*
Margareta Akermark, *Associate Director*

The Museum of Modern Art Film Library, founded in 1935, is an educational institution which collects and preserves representative motion pictures and related materials, with the object of making them available for study.

The three thousand titles and twelve million feet of film in the library's collection include feature films, films of record, advertising and propaganda films, experimental and animated films from all countries which have a major film industry. The films date from 1894 to the present. It is perhaps the most important international collection outside of government-owned archives. The library's circulating programs provide films to over two thousand educational institutions, museums, and film societies throughout the United States and Canada. Nine series of programs are now available to subscribers. These provide a professional review of the history and the technical and esthetic development of the motion picture, from its invention until recent years, in this country and abroad. They are approximately two hours long and are usually preceded by explanatory comment. The Film Library has prepared piano scores for the majority of its silent films. These are available upon request—and in advance of the films to provide sufficient time for rehearsal.

In 1938 the Film Library joined with the British Film Institute, the Cinémathèque Française, and the Reichsfilmarchiv, to form the International Federation of Film Archives, an organization which now has affiliates in more than thirty-five countries. Separate films and series of motion pictures are exchanged between the Film Library and member institutions of the International Federation.

The library conducts an active program of regular daily film screenings in its main auditorium in New York City. In addition, the museum contains a private projection room for small groups, and recently space was allocated for a study room equipped to permit hand-viewing of films by the staff and outside scholars and researchers. Some of the film series screened for the public in 1965 included *Recent Spanish Films* (selected by the Associate Director in cooperation with Uniespana and the Motion Picture Association of America); *Films of D. W. Griffith* (the most comprehensive exhibit of Griffith's work ever held); *Films of Stanley Kubrick; Films of Joseph Von Sternberg; The Independent Film* (selections from the Film-Makers Cooperative).

The Film Library sponsors a variety of lectures and symposia on films and film making, publishes books and pamphlets relating to motion pictures and film artists, arranges special exhibits of motion-picture stills, and maintains an active (within strict financial limits) program of film preservation.

Public Libraries

During the last twenty years a number of public libraries, particularly libraries in large urban areas, have established audio-visual divisions which collect 16-mm. motion pictures and make them available for screening. Those who have succeeded in establishing film programs in these institutions have done so against heavy odds. Libraries which profess to offer enlightenment through the use of a full range of materials were nonetheless established to encourage *reading* and a better understanding of the *printed word*. The introduction of film has disturbed both prejudices and systems.

Changes have been made, of course, but taking the country as a whole, these changes are not yet profound. For even in the most enterprising film divisions, there are severe restrictions upon the kinds of films which may be acquired and shown in public screening programs. Typically, there are prohibitions against the acquisition of "entertainment" films. (Imagine these libraries banishing novels and other forms of fiction because they are entertaining.) Acquiring an impressive collection of motion pictures is an expensive procedure, and in most cases funds for this purpose must be drawn from money set aside for more conventional expenditures. Obviously, some librarians have neither the taste nor the training for selecting films. How else can we explain why many library film collections are stuffed with incredibly dull and generally uninformative films, foisted chiefly upon groups of children in the hope that they will prove helpful as well as mildly diverting? Whether the unimaginative people (often it's a committee) who choose these films want to face up to it or not, dull pictures "explaining" personal hygiene will always receive precisely the kind of reception they deserve.

But there are exceptions: the Donnell Branch of the New York Public Library, the Enoch Pratt Library in Baltimore, the public libraries in Dallas, Los Angeles, and Dearborn, Michigan, to name a few. It is often through such institutions that the serious film student has an opportunity to see important motion pictures of the past, or films screened in sequence in order to demonstrate the development of film-making technique.

The Los Angeles Library's collection of some one thousand titles includes a special Film Study Collection, developed to provide students and film makers with rare or esoteric film material. Annotations in the general catalogue call attention to special techniques in specific films and important production credits. Over a third of the motion-picture circulation in Los Angeles is carried on through branch libraries—in a city occupying more than four hundred and fifty square miles and with a population of over three million.

In its 1963–64 Film Catalogue, the Donnell Branch of the New York Public Library (in which most of the library's motion-picture activities have been consolidated) lists about thirty films under the topic "Films as Art," including *Begone Dull Care, Dream of the Wild Horses, Liquid Jazz,* and *N.Y., N.Y.* Series of noon hour screenings in the Donnell Branch's midtown 278-seat auditorium provide a showcase of new films, virtually all of them nontheatrical. Evening programs such as "New Concepts in Music for Films," demonstrate production techniques through lectures and screenings.

The Enoch Pratt Free Library in Baltimore, which circulates its films throughout the entire state of Maryland, includes in its collection a "History of the Motion Picture Series" (classics of the silent screen presented in edited form—*Dr. Jekell and Mr. Hyde; The Fun Factory*—Sennett excerpts; *The Hunchback of Notre Dame; The Sad Clowns*—Chaplin, Keaton, and Langton; *The Thief of Bagdad;* etc.) and other films which comment on movies and movie making; e.g., *The Golden Age of Comedy*—comedians of the 20's, *Movies on the March, Origins of the Motion Picture, Sergei Eisenstein* (produced by Central Documentary Film Studios in Moscow). The Enoch Pratt Library has also sponsored a series of screenings on "The Film Makers," using movies from its own collection, including those of Alain Resnais, Satyajit Ray, Jack Clayton, Lindsey Anderson, Luis Bunuel, and Roman Polanski.

The Audio-Visual Department of the Dallas Public Library has been operating for nearly twenty-five years. Its film collection of about two thousand titles has occasionally been employed in the development of special series on "Film Makers, presenting the motion picture as a medium of expression for various types of productions within specific subject areas . . . ," programs which have featured films by Francis Thompson, Norman McLaren, Albert Lamorisse, and others.

One of the most venturesome public library collections of motion pictures is located in Dearborn, Michigan, where films in the library's catalogue are described as "informational and *cultural.*" The introduction to this catalogue explains to potential borrowers, "Many moviegoers have been *watching* movies for years but very few have really *seen* them." The Dearborn Library lists over one hundred titles in its "History of Motion Pictures" and "Experimental Films" categories. Considerable attention is also given to motion pictures interpreting the art of film editing and screen writing, the versatility of film music, color in movies, documentary pictures, and so on; all relatively unsophisticated for the hard-core film buff, but miles ahead of most libraries which make no attempt to interpret the motion-picture medium.

Film Societies

It would be too much to say that the establishment of a campus film society always precedes the initiation of a formal film-study course. But there is certainly more than a casual relationship between the two enterprises. Film societies provide, somewhat haphazardly, an extremely valuable source of better-than-average motion pictures (both foreign and domestic) as well as information *about* films.

There are about four thousand active film societies in the United States. The total audience attending their screenings is roughly 2.5 million people annually. According to the American Federation of Film Societies (A.F.F.S.)—which is briefly described in Appendix B—about twenty-five hundred of the local societies are satisfied to present programs which are characterized by an emphasis upon diverting the audience. In addition, A.F.F.S. has identified about one thousand "serious groups" whose film programs are designed to present movies in some kind of ordered, though perhaps idiosyncratic, fashion; programs which are meant to instruct as well as entertain. The majority of these are on college campuses.

As film societies mature and become increasingly sophisticated, their programs usually reflect an interest in specialized series. These may trace varying currents and fashions in film making, the latest examples of films from specific countries, or some film genre such as the poetic documentary, realist cinema, the western, the samurai film, musicals, or propaganda films. Today, greater interest is being placed on the retrospective series which features the work of one actor or director.

Although the screening itself is central to all film series, most societies also schedule lectures presented by visiting film artists or critics, hold panel discussions and informal seminars, and distribute large volumes of program notes. A.F.F.S. has established a program note exchange service, maintained by volunteer assistance at Dartmouth Films, Dartmouth College, in Hanover, New Hampshire. In order to be eligible to receive the notes, each member society must supply the exchange with a few hundred copies of the notes it has prepared. About two thousand films are "covered" by the notes in the A.F.F.S./Dartmouth exchange file. Their completeness and quality is uneven but the service nevertheless represents a highly important source of information in a country which has given little attention to film documentation.

APPENDIX D

Tables

The following tables have been prepared by Donald E. Staples, Assistant Professor, The Ohio State University, as part of a project supervised by Professor Jack C. Ellis of Northwestern University. The tables, first published in the *Educational Record*,[1] have been subsequently revised by Professor Staples for this publication.

TABLE 1: NUMBER OF FILM COURSES IN THE 100 LARGEST COLLEGES AND UNIVERSITIES, BY APPROACH TO CONTENT, 1963–64

School	*Audio-Visual*	*Production*	*History, Criticism, Appreciation*	*Communication*	*Total*
University of Southern California	7	28	14	13	62
University of California	8	34	18	0	60
Boston University	11	10	11	8	40
Indiana University	14	4	1	12	31
Columbia University	3	15	4	7	29
New York University	4	15	4	4	27
San Francisco State College	4	10	6	6	26
Northwestern University	3	6	5	7	21
Michigan State University	5	7	4	5	21
University of North Carolina	1	11	3	5	20
University of Minnesota	6	4	4	4	18
University of Miami	2	10	1	3	16
University of Iowa	5	4	3	4	16
Baylor University	4	10	2	0	16
Syracuse University	8	3	3	1	15
University of Wisconsin	6	2	5	1	14
Kent State University	8	3	0	2	13
Pennsylvania State University	7	2	4	0	13
Southern Methodist University	2	6	5	0	13
Stanford University	2	3	3	4	12
Ohio State University	4	4	3	1	12
University of Oklahoma	6	5	0	1	12
City College (City University of New York)	0	6	3	2	11
California State College at Long Beach	4	3	2	1	10
University of Denver	5	3	1	1	10
Wayne State University	9	0	0	1	10
Oklahoma State University	5	2	1	2	10
Brigham Young University	1	2	2	4	9
University of Washington	5	2	1	1	9
San Jose State College	4	1	1	2	8
University of Illinois	3	2	2	1	8
University of Houston	0	7	1	0	8
University of Texas	3	2	0	3	8
West Virginia University	5	3	0	0	8
Auburn University	4	1	1	1	7
Los Angeles City College	0	6	0	1	7
University of Connecticut	4	2	1	0	7
University of Detroit	2	2	1	2	7

[1] *Educational Record,* Winter 1965 (Washington: American Council on Education, 1965), pp. 64–67.

TABLE 1—*continued*

School	*Audio-Visual*	*Production*	*History, Criticism, Appreciation*	*Communication*	*Total*
University of Georgia	3	2	1	1	7
Cornell University	1	1	3	2	7
Texas Technological College	5	1	1	0	7
Marquette University	2	2	2	1	7
University of Florida	2	4	0	0	6
Purdue University	4	1	1	0	6
Temple University	2	2	1	1	6
Western Reserve University	5	0	1	0	6
University of Kentucky	4	1	1	0	6
University of Oregon	3	0	2	1	6
University of Pennsylvania	3	1	1	1	6
University of Utah	4	1	1	0	6
University of Colorado	5	0	0	0	5
Florida State University	5	0	0	0	5
University of Notre Dame	1	2	2	0	5
Iowa State University	2	2	0	1	5
University of Maryland	4	0	1	0	5
University of Michigan	3	2	0	0	5
Seton Hall University	2	2	0	1	5
St. John's University (New York)	5	0	0	0	5
University of Kansas	0	1	2	1	4
Louisiana State University	3	1	0	0	4
University of Nebraska	3	1	0	0	4
Rutgers—The State University	2	0	0	2	4
State University of New York at Buffalo	2	0	2	0	4
Washington State University	1	2	1	0	4
University of Alabama	0	1	2	0	3
University of Arizona	2	0	0	1	3
Kansas State University	2	1	0	0	3
Johns Hopkins University	1	0	2	0	3
Harvard University	0	0	2	1	3
University of Missouri	2	0	0	1	3
University of Rochester	3	0	0	0	3
Oregon State University	2	0	0	1	3
University of Pittsburgh	3	0	0	0	3
University of Tennessee	3	0	0	0	3
North Texas State University	3	0	0	0	3
Loyola University (Illinois)	1	0	0	1	2
Roosevelt University	2	0	0	0	2
University of Louisville	1	0	0	1	2
Tulane University	0	1	0	1	2
Fordham University	0	1	1	0	2
Hunter College	1	0	0	1	2
Duke University	1	0	0	1	2
Ohio University	0	1	1	0	2
Texas A&M University	1	1	0	0	2
George Washington University	1	0	0	0	1
De Paul University	1	0	0	0	1
Illinois Inst. of Tech.	0	1	0	0	1
University of Chicago	1	0	0	0	1
Boston College	1	0	0	0	1
Saint Louis University	1	0	0	0	1
Washington University	0	1	0	0	1
Brooklyn College	0	0	1	0	1
Pace College	0	0	1	0	1
Miami University	1	0	0	0	1
University of Cincinnati	1	0	0	0	1
Yale University	0	0	0	0	0
Georgetown University	0	0	0	0	0
Massachusetts Inst. of Tech.	0	0	0	0	0
Northeastern University	0	0	0	0	0
Polytechnic Institute of Brooklyn	0	0	0	0	0
Total	286	276	152	132	846

TABLE 2: Sponsoring Departments of Film Courses in the 100 Largest Colleges and Universities

Department	*1952–53*	*1964–65*	*Net Gain*
Education	217	264	47
Theater arts; dramatic arts; drama; speech; speech and dramatic art.	97	138	41
Radio and television; telecommunications; radio, television, and motion pictures; radio; television	13	149	136
Communication(s); communication arts; communications in education	29	81	52
Journalism	42	57	15
Library science; library training; library service	24	52	28
Motion pictures; cinema; films	71	47	−24
Sociology; social relations	16	14	−2
Fine arts; art	8	14	6
Photography; photography and film	13	10	−3
English	14	8	−6
Music	12	7	−5
Political science; government	7	4	−3
Marketing; advertising; publicity	5	1	−4
Psychology	5	0	−5
Philosophy	2	0	−2
Total	575	846	271

TABLE 3: Film History, Criticism, and Appreciation Courses of the 100 Largest Colleges and Universities, by State

State	*Number*	*State*	*Number*
California	44	Maryland	3
New York	22	North Carolina	3
Massachusetts	13	Utah	3
Texas	9	Kansas	2
Illinois	7	Oregon	2
Wisconsin	7	Washington	2
Pennsylvania	6	Colorado	1
Michigan	5	Connecticut	1
Indiana	4	Florida	1
Minnesota	4	Georgia	1
Ohio	4	Kentucky	1
Alabama	3	Oklahoma	1
Iowa	3		
		Total	152

TABLE 4: FILM HISTORY, CRITICISM, AND APPRECIATION COURSES OF THE 100 LARGEST COLLEGES AND UNIVERSITIES, BY SPONSORING DEPARTMENT

Department	*Number*	*Department*	*Number*
Theater arts, etc.	58	Fine arts	6
Radio and television, etc.	30	Education	3
Communication (s), etc.	22	English	3
Journalism	15	Photography, etc.	2
Motion pictures, etc.	11	Music	2
		Total	152

BIBLIOGRAPHY

A SELECTED BIBLIOGRAPHY

GENERAL

HOUSTON, PENELOPE. *The Contemporary Cinema.* Harmondsworth, Middlesex: Penguin Books Inc., 1963.

HUGHES, ROBERT (ed.). *Film: Book 1.* New York: Grove Press, Inc., 1959.

JACOBS, LEWIS (ed.). *Introduction to the Art of the Movies.* New York: Farrar, Straus and Co., 1960.

KNIGHT, ARTHUR. *The Liveliest Art.* New York: New American Library of World Literature, 1959.

LAWSON, JOHN HOWARD. *Film: The Creative Process.* New York: Hill & Wang, Inc., 1964.

MANVELL, ROGER. *Films.* New York: Cambridge University Press; Harmondsworth, Middlesex: Penguin Books Inc., 1950.

———. *The Film and the Public.* Harmondsworth, Middlesex: Penguin Books Inc., 1955.

ROTHA, PAUL. *Rotha on the Film.* New York: Oxford University Press; London: Faber and Faber, 1958.

SCHMIDT, GEORGE; SCHMALENBACH, WERNER; and BACHLIN, PETER. *The Film: Its Economic, Social, and Artistic Problems.* London: Falcon, 1948.

TALBOT, DANIEL (ed.). *Film: An Anthology.* New York: Simon and Schuster, Inc., 1959. (Berkeley: University of California Press, 1966, paperback.)

TAYLOR, JOHN RUSSELL. *Cinema Eye, Cinema Ear.* New York: Hill & Wang, Inc., 1965.

AESTHETICS

ARNHEIM, RUDOLF. *Film as Art.* Berkeley: University of California Press, 1957.

BALASZ, BÉLA. *Theory of the Film.* New York: Roy Publishers, Inc., 1953.

BENOIT-LEVY, JEAN. *The Art of the Motion Picture.* New York: Coward-McCann, Inc., 1946.

BLUESTONE, GEORGE. *Novels into Film.* Berkeley: University of California Press, 1961.

COCTEAU, JEAN. *Cocteau on the Film.* New York: Roy Publishers, Inc., 1954.

DEREN, MAYA. *An Anagram of Ideas on Art, Form and Film.* Yonkers, New York: Alicat Book Shop Press, 1946.

EISENSTEIN, SERGEI. *Film Form.* New York: Harcourt, Brace and World, Inc., 1949.

———. *The Film Sense.* New York: Harcourt, Brace and World, Inc., 1942.

———. *Notes of a Film Director.* London: Lawrence and Wishart, 1959.

FELDMAN, JOSEPH, and FELDMAN, HARRY. *Dynamics of the Film.* New York: Hermitage House, 1952.

GRIERSON, JOHN. *Grierson on Documentary.* Edited and compiled by Forsyth Hardy. New York: Harcourt, Brace and World, Inc., 1947. (Berkeley: University of California Press, 1966.)

KRACAUER, SIEGFRIED. *Theory of Film.* New York: Oxford University Press, 1960.

LINDGREN, ERNEST. *The Art of the Film* (Rev. ed.). New York: Macmillan Co., 1963.

PUDOVKIN, V. I. *Film Technique and Film Acting.* New York: British Book Centre, Inc.; New York: Lear, 1954.

SPOTTISWOODE, RAYMOND. *A Grammar of the Film.* Berkeley: University of California Press, 1950.

WILLIAMS, RAYMOND, and ORROM, MICHAEL. *Preface to Film.* London: Film Drama, 1954.

CRITICISM AND REVIEWS

AGEE, JAMES. *Agee on Film.* New York: McDowell, Obelensky Inc., 1958.

HILLS, JANET. *Fragments: Janet Hills, 1919–1956.* London: Privately published, 1956.

KAEL, PAULINE. *I Lost it At the Movies.* Boston: Atlantic Monthly Press, Inc.–Little, Brown and Co., 1965.

LEJEUNE, C. A. *Chestnuts in Her Lap, 1936–1946.* London: Phoenix, 1947.

MANVELL, ROGER and others (eds.). *Shots in the Dark.* New York: British Book Centre, Inc.; London: Allan Wingate, 1952.

WARSHOW, ROBERT. *The Immediate Experience.* New York: Doubleday & Co., Inc., 1962.

WINNINGTON, RICHARD. *Drawn and Quartered.* London: Saturn, 1948.

ZINSSER, WILLIAM K. *Seen Any Good Movies Lately?* Garden City, New York: Doubleday & Co., Inc., 1958.

PERIODICALS

Films are regularly reviewed in the following periodicals: *America, The Commonweal, Esquire, New Republic, The New Yorker, Newsweek, The Saturday Review, Time.* The periodicals listed below cover a wide range of critical opinion. For teachers new to a film study, *Screen Education* and *Film Quarterly* will probably be the most readable and most useful.

Cahiers Du Cinéma (English Edition). 635 Madison Ave., New York, New York 10022. Monthly. $9.50.

Catholic Film Newsletter. National Legion of Decency, 453 Madison Ave., New York, New York. $5.00 per year.

Cinema. 9641 Santa Monica Blvd., Beverly Hills, California. $4.50.

Film Comment. 11 St. Luke's Pl., New York, New York 10014. $2.75 per year.

Film Culture. GPO Box 1499, New York, New York. $3.00.

Film Facts. P.O. Box 53, Village Station, 150 Christopher St., New York, New York.

Film Heritage. Box 42, University of Dayton, Dayton, Ohio 45409. Quarterly. $2.00 per year.

Film News. 250 West 57th St., New York, New York 10019. $4.00.

Film Quarterly. University of California Press, Berkeley, California 94704. $4.00.

Film Society Review. 144 Bleecker St., New York, New York 10012. (Included in A.F.F.S. membership fee.)

Films and Filming. 33s 154 Queen St., Portsmouth, England.

Films in Review. 31 Union Square, New York, New York. $6.00.

Green Sheet. 522 Fifth Ave., New York, New York. Free to organizations.

Motion Picture Herald. 1270 Sixth Ave., New York, New York. Biweekly. $5.00.

New York Film Bulletin. 116 East 60th St., New York, New York. $3.00 per year.

Screen Education. Society for Education in Film and Television in the United States, c/o School of Public Relations and Communications, Boston University, Boston, Massachusetts 02115. $5.00.

Sight and Sound. 255 Seventh Ave., New York, New York. $3.50.

Variety. 154 West 46th St., New York, New York. 52 issues. $12.00.